FREE DVD

From Stress to Success DVD from Trivium Test Prep

Dear Customer,

Thank you for purchasing from Cirrus Test Prep! Whether you're looking to join the military, get into college, or advance your career, we're honored to be a part of your journey.

To show our appreciation (and to help you relieve a little of that test prep stress), we're offering a **FREE** ***ParaProfessional Essential Test Tips DVD**** by Cirrus Test Prep. Our DVD includes 35 test preparation strategies that will help keep you calm and collected before and during your big exam. All we ask is that you email us your feedback and describe your experience with our product. Amazing, awful, or just so-so: we want to hear what you have to say!

To receive your **FREE** ***ParaProfessional Essential Test Tips DVD***, please email us at 5star@cirrustestprep.com. Include "Free 5 Star" in the subject line and the following information in your email:

1. The title of the product you purchased.
2. Your rating from 1 – 5 (with 5 being the best).
3. Your feedback about the product, including how our materials helped you meet your goals and ways in which we can improve our products.
4. Your full name and shipping address so we can send your **FREE** ***ParaProfessional Essential Test Tips DVD***.

If you have any questions or concerns please feel free to contact us directly at 5star@cirrustestprep.com.

Thank you, and good luck with your studies!

* Please note that the free DVD is <u>not included</u> with this book. To receive the free DVD, please follow the instructions above.

ParaProfessional Study Guide

ParaPro Assessment Review Book with Practice Test Questions for the ParaProfessional Exam

Copyright © 2019 by Cirrus Test Prep

ALL RIGHTS RESERVED. By purchase of this book, you have been licensed one copy for personal use only. No part of this work may be reproduced, redistributed, or used in any form or by any means without prior written permission of the publisher and copyright owner. Cirrus Test Prep; Trivium Test Prep; Accepted, Inc.; and Ascencia Test Prep are all imprints of Trivium Test Prep, LLC.

ETS was not involved in the creation or production of this product, is not in any way affiliated with Cirrus Test Prep, and does not sponsor or endorse this product. All test names (and their acronyms) are trademarks of their respective owners. This study guide is for general information only and does not claim endorsement by any third party.

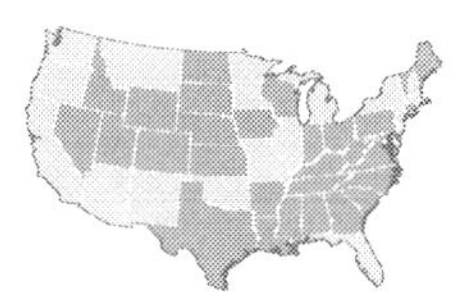

Table of Contents

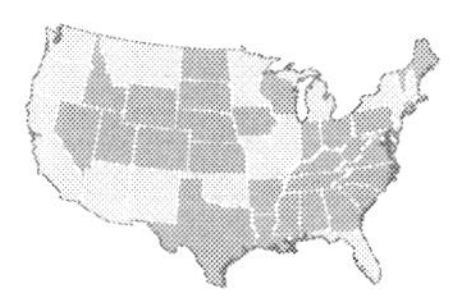

Online Resources

To help you fully prepare for your Praxis ParaPro Assessment (1755) exam, Cirrus includes online resources with the purchase of this study guide.

Practice Test

In addition to the practice test included in this book, we also offer an online exam. Since many exams today are computer-based, getting to practice your test-taking skills on the computer is a great way to prepare.

Flash Cards

A convenient supplement to this study guide, Cirrus's e-flash cards enable you to review important terms easily on your computer or smartphone.

From Stress to Success

Watch *From Stress to Success*, a brief but insightful YouTube video that offers the tips, tricks, and secrets experts use to score higher on the exam.

Reviews

Leave a review, send us helpful feedback, or sign up for Cirrus's promotions—including free books!

To access these materials, please enter the following URL into your browser:

www.cirrustestprep.com/parapro-online-resources.

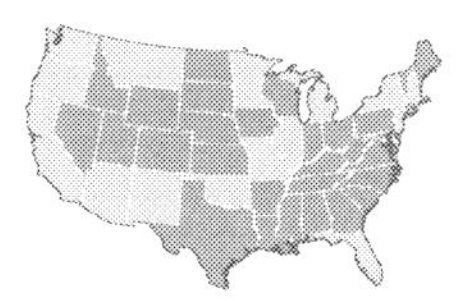

Introduction

Congratulations on choosing to take the Praxis ParaPro Assessment (1755) exam! By purchasing this book, you've taken the first step toward becoming a paraprofessional.

This guide will provide you with a detailed overview of the Praxis ParaPro exam, so you know exactly what to expect on test day. We'll take you through all the concepts covered on the test and give you the opportunity to test your knowledge with practice questions. Even if it's been a while since you last took a major test, don't worry; we'll make sure you're more than ready!

What is the Praxis ParaPro Assessment (1755)?

Praxis Series tests are a part of teaching licensure in approximately forty states. Each state uses the tests and scores in different ways, so be sure to check the certification requirements in your state by going to www.ets.org/praxis/states. There, you will find information detailing the role of the Praxis tests in determining teaching certification in your state, what scores are required, and how to transfer Praxis scores from one state to another.

What's on the Praxis ParaPro Assessment (1755)?

The content in this guide will prepare you for the Praxis ParaPro Assessment (1755). This test assesses whether you possess the knowledge and skills necessary to become a paraprofessional. You have a maximum of 150 minutes to complete the entire test. The test always has a total of ninety selected-response questions; however, the number of questions specific to each subject is approximate (see the table below).

In each content area—reading, math, and writing—about two-thirds of the questions will test your basic skills and knowledge of the content itself. The rest of the questions address applying that knowledge in the classroom.

Praxis ParaPro Assessment (1755) Content		
Subjects	**Approximate Number of Questions**	**Percentage of Test**
Reading	30	33 1/3%
Mathematics	30	33 1/3%
Writing	30	33 1/3%
Total	90 questions	150 minutes (2.5 hours)

Reading

You will answer approximately thirty multiple-choice questions (1/3 of the test) on reading. You will be tested on your ability to analyze passages. Expect to identify the main and supporting ideas in a passage, make inferences about a passage, discuss organization of passages, and differentiate facts from opinions. You will also need to interpret visual information from charts or graphs.

Approximately one-third of the reading questions will cover classroom situations. You'll need to show you can help students with skills like learning vocabulary, sounding out words, using prereading strategies, and consulting the dictionary.

Mathematics

You will answer approximately thirty multiple-choice questions (1/3 of the test) on mathematics. You should expect instruction questions to cover three main areas: number sense and basic algebra, geometry and measurement, and data analysis.

- Number sense and basic algebra questions test your arithmetic skills, including place value, percentages, order of operations, mental math, word problems, and basic linear equations.
- Geometry and measurement questions ask about representations of time and money (fractions and decimals), unit conversions, identifying basic shapes and determining their area, perimeter, and volume, and graphing data on a coordinate plane.
- Data analysis questions ask you to interpret information from graphic sources, create basic tables and graphs, and compute mean, median, and mode.

About one-third of the math questions test your ability to assist the teacher in the classroom. You may NOT use a calculator on the test.

WRITING

You will answer approximately thirty multiple-choice questions (1/3 of the test) on writing. Questions will ask you to identify errors in grammar, punctuation, word usage, and spelling. You will also be asked to identify the parts of a sentence and parts of speech.

Approximately one-third of the writing questions will cover writing in the classroom. These questions will focus on specific scenarios typically faced by the paraprofessional when working with students. You'll need to show you can help students with prewriting strategies, drafting and editing, writing for different audiences, and writing in different modes.

HOW IS THE PRAXIS PARAPRO ASSESSMENT (1755) SCORED?

The questions are equally weighted. Keep in mind that some multiple-choice questions are experimental questions for the purpose of the Praxis test-writers and will not count toward your overall score. However, since those questions are not indicated on the test, you must respond to every question. There is no penalty for guessing on Praxis tests, so be sure to eliminate answer choices and answer every question. If you still do not know the answer, guess; you may get it right!

There is no single passing score for the ParaPro: each state or credentialing agency determines its passing score in cooperation with ETS (Educational Testing Service). So check with your state or institution to find out what minimum passing score it requires for certification.

In many states, scores are automatically sent to the state credentialing agency. Check with ETS to determine if this applies in your state. Your score report will be available on your Praxis account for ten years. Your score will be available immediately after the test.

HOW IS THE PRAXIS PARAPRO ASSESSMENT (1755) ADMINISTERED?

The Praxis Series tests are available at testing centers across the nation. To find a testing center near you, go to http://www.ets.org/praxis/register. At this site, you can create a Praxis account, check testing dates, register for a test, or find instructions for registering via mail or phone. The Praxis ParaPro Assessment (1755) is administered as a computerized test. The Praxis website allows you to take a practice test to acclimate yourself to the computerized format.

On the day of your test, be sure to bring your admission ticket (which is provided when you register) and photo ID. The testing facility will provide pencils and erasers and an area outside of the testing room to store your personal belongings. You are allowed no personal effects in the testing area. Cellphones and other electronic, photographic, recording, or listening devices are not permitted in the testing center at all, and bringing those items may be cause for dismissal, forfeiture of your testing fees, and cancellation of your scores. As mentioned above, you may NOT use a calculator on the ParaPro. For more details on what is and is not permitted at your testing center, refer to http://www.ets.org/praxis/test_day/bring or the ETS ParaPro Assessment Information Bulletin.

About Cirrus Test Prep

Cirrus Test Prep study guides are designed by current and former educators and are tailored to meet your needs as an incoming educator. Our guides offer all of the resources necessary to help you pass certification tests across the nation.

Cirrus clouds are graceful, wispy clouds characterized by their high altitude. Just like cirrus clouds, Cirrus Test Prep's goal is to help educators "aim high" when it comes to obtaining their certification and entering the classroom.

About This Guide

This guide will help you master the most important test topics and also develop critical test-taking skills. We have built features into our books to prepare you for your tests and increase your score. Along with a detailed summary of the test's format, content, and scoring, we offer an in-depth overview of the content knowledge required to pass the test. Our sidebars provide interesting information, highlight key concepts, and review content so that you can solidify your understanding of the exam's concepts. Test your knowledge with sample questions and detailed answer explanations in the text that help you think through the problems on the exam as well as practice test questions that reflect the content and format of the ParaPro. We're pleased you've chosen Cirrus to be a part of your professional journey!

Reading Skills and Knowledge

The Main Idea

The **main idea** of a text is the argument that the author is trying to make about a particular **topic**. Every sentence in a passage should support or address the main idea in some way.

Identifying the Main Idea

Consider a political election. A candidate is running for office and plans to deliver a speech asserting her position on tax reform, which is that taxes should be lowered. The topic of the speech is tax reform, and the main idea is that taxes should be lowered. The candidate is going to assert this in her speech, and support it with examples proving why lowering taxes would benefit the public and how it could be accomplished.

Other candidates may have different perspectives on the same topic; they may believe that higher taxes are necessary, or that current taxes are adequate. It is likely that their speeches, while on the same topic of tax reform, would have different main ideas supported by different examples and evidence.

> HELPFUL HINT
>
> **Topic:** The subject of the passage. **Main idea:** The argument the writer is making about the topic.

Let's look at an example passage to see how to identify the topic and main idea.

> Babe Didrikson Zaharias, one of the most decorated female athletes of the twentieth century, is an inspiration for everyone. Born in 1911 in Beaumont, Texas, Zaharias lived in a time when women were considered second class to men, but she never let that stop her from becoming a champion. Zaharias was one of seven children in a poor immigrant family and was competitive from an early age. As a child she excelled at most

things she tried, especially sports, which continued into high school and beyond. After high school, Zaharias played amateur basketball for two years, and soon after began training in track and field. Despite the fact that women were only allowed to enter in three events, Zaharias represented the United States in the 1932 Los Angeles Olympics, and won two gold medals and one silver in track and field events.

The topic of this paragraph is obviously Babe Zaharias—the whole passage describes events from her life. Determining the main idea, however, requires a little more analysis. To figure out the main idea, consider what the writer is saying about Zaharias. The passage describes her life, but the main idea of the paragraph is what it says about her accomplishments. The writer is saying that she is someone to admire. That is the main idea and what unites all the information in the paragraph.

SAMPLE QUESTION

From so far away it's easy to imagine the surface of our solar system's planets as enigmas—how could we ever know what those far-flung planets really look like? It turns out, however, that scientists have a number of tools at their disposal that allow them to paint detailed pictures of many planets' surfaces. The topography of Venus, for example, has been explored by several space probes, including the Russian Venera landers and NASA's Magellan orbiter. In addition to these long-range probes, NASA has also used its series of "Great Observatories" to study distant planets. These four massively powerful orbiting telescopes are the famous Hubble Space Telescope, the Compton Gamma Ray Observatory, the Chandra X-Ray Observatory, and the Spitzer Space Telescope. Such powerful telescopes aren't just found in space: NASA makes use of Earth-based telescopes as well. Scientists at the National Radio Astronomy Observatory in Charlottesville, Virginia, have spent decades using radio imaging to build an incredibly detailed portrait of Venus's surface.

1) **Which of the following sentences best describes the main idea of the passage?**

    A. It is impossible to know what the surfaces of other planets are really like.

    B. Telescopes are an important tool for scientists studying planets in our solar system.

    C. Venus's surface has many of the same features as Earth's, including volcanoes, craters, and channels.

    D. Scientists use a variety of advanced technologies to study the surfaces of the planets in our solar system.

Topic and Summary Sentences

The topic, and sometimes the main idea of a paragraph, is introduced in the **topic sentence**. The topic sentence usually appears early in a passage. The first sentence in the example paragraph above about Babe Zaharias states the topic and main idea: *Babe Didrikson Zaharias, one of the most decorated female athletes of the twentieth century, is an inspiration for everyone.*

Even though paragraphs generally begin with topic sentences, on occasion writers build up to the topic sentence by using supporting details in order to generate interest or construct an argument. Be alert for paragraphs in which writers do not include a clear topic sentence.

There may also be a **summary sentence** at the end of a passage. As its name suggests, this sentence sums up the passage, often by restating the main idea and the author's key evidence supporting it.

> The Constitution of the United States establishes a series of limits to rein in centralized power. "Separation of powers" distributes federal authority among three branches: the executive, the legislative, and the judicial. "Checks and balances" allow the branches to prevent any one branch from usurping power. "States' rights" are protected under the Constitution from too much encroachment by the federal government. "Enumeration of powers" names the specific and few powers the federal government has. These four restrictions have helped sustain the American republic for over two centuries.

SAMPLE QUESTION

2) **Which of the following is the passage's topic sentence?**

   A. These four restrictions have helped sustain the American republic for over two centuries.

   B. The Constitution of the United States establishes a series of limits to rein in centralized power.

   C. "Enumeration of powers" names the specific and few powers the federal government has.

   D. "Checks and balances" allow the branches to prevent any one branch from usurping power.

SUPPORTING DETAILS

Supporting details reinforce the author's main idea. Let's look again at the passage about athlete Babe Zaharias.

> Babe Didrikson Zaharias, one of the most decorated female athletes of the twentieth century, is an inspiration for everyone. Born in 1911 in Beaumont, Texas, Zaharias lived in a time when women were considered second class to men, but she never let that stop her from becoming a champion. Babe was one of seven children in a poor immigrant family and was competitive from an early age. As a child she excelled at most things

> she tried, especially sports, which continued into high school and beyond. After high school, Babe played amateur basketball for two years, and soon after began training in track and field. Despite the fact that women were only allowed to enter in three events, Zaharias represented the United States in the 1932 Los Angeles Olympics, and won two gold medals and one silver for track and field events.

Remember that the main idea of the passage is that Zaharias is someone to admire—an idea introduced in the opening sentence. The remainder of the paragraph provides details that support this assertion. These details include the circumstances of her childhood, her childhood success at sports, and the medals she won at the Olympics.

When looking for supporting details, be alert for *signal words*. These signal words tell you that a supporting fact or idea will follow, and so can be helpful in identifying supporting details. Signal words can also help you rule out certain sentences as the main idea or topic sentence. If a sentence begins with one of these phrases, it will likely be too specific to be a main idea.

HELPFUL HINT

Signal words:

- for example
- specifically
- in addition
- furthermore
- for instance
- others
- in particular
- some

SAMPLE QUESTIONS

From so far away it's easy to imagine the surface of our solar system's planets as enigmas—how could we ever know what those far-flung planets really look like? It turns out, however, that scientists have a number of tools at their disposal that allow them to paint detailed pictures of many planets' surfaces. The topography of Venus, for example, has been explored by several space probes, including the Russian Venera landers and NASA's Magellan orbiter. In addition to these long-range probes, NASA has also used its series of orbiting telescopes to study distant planets. These four massively powerful telescopes include the famous Hubble Space Telescope as well as the Compton Gamma Ray Observatory, the Chandra X-Ray Observatory, and the Spitzer Space Telescope. Such powerful telescopes aren't just found in space: NASA makes use of Earth-based telescopes as well. Scientists at the National Radio Astronomy Observatory in Charlottesville, Virginia, have spent decades using radio imaging to build an incredibly detailed portrait of Venus's surface.

3) According to the passage, which of the following is a space probe used to explore the surface of Venus?

A. *Magellan* orbiter

B. Hubble Space Telescope

C. Spitzer Space Telescope

D. National Radio Astronomy Observatory

4) If true, which detail could be added to the passage above to support the author's argument that scientists use many different technologies to study the surface of planets?

A. Because Earth's atmosphere blocks X-rays, gamma rays, and infrared radiation, NASA needed to put telescopes in orbit above the atmosphere.

B. In 2015, NASA released a map of Venus that was created by compiling images from orbiting telescopes and long-range space probes.

C. NASA is currently using the *Curiosity* and *Opportunity* rovers to look for signs of ancient life on Mars.

D. NASA has spent over $2.5 billion to build, launch, and repair the Hubble Space Telescope.

ORGANIZATION OF PASSAGES

Some reading questions on the ParaPro will ask you about how reading passages are organized. To identify the structural organization of a passage, look at the order in which the author presents information and the transitions used to connect those pieces. Specific text structures are described in the table below.

Table 1.1 Text Structure

Name	Structure	Words to Look For
Cause and effect	The author describes a situation and then its effects.	because, as a result, consequently, therefore, for this reason
Compare and contrast	The author explores the similarities and differences between two or more things.	similarly, like, in addition, however, alternatively, unlike, but
Problem and solution	The author presents a problem and offers a solution.	if...then, problem, solution, answer
Description	The author describes a thing or process.	for example, for instance, such as, to illustrate
Chronological	The author lists events in the order in which they happened.	first, second, next, after, before

SAMPLE QUESTION

In an effort to increase women's presence in government, several countries in Latin America, including Argentina, Brazil, and Mexico, have implemented legislated candidate quotas. These quotas require that at least 30 percent of a party's candidate list in any election cycle consists of women who have a legitimate chance at election. As a result, Latin America has the greatest number of female heads of government in the world, and the second highest percentage of female members of parliament after Nordic Europe. However, these trends do not carry over outside of politics. While 25 percent of legislators in Latin America are now women, less than 2 percent of CEOs in the region are female.

5) **Which of the following best describes the organization of the passage?**
   A. compare and contrast
   B. chronological
   C. cause and effect
   D. description

Making Inferences

Part of analyzing a passage is anticipating what other information could logically be added to the passage. For example, in a nonfiction passage on the ParaPro, you might be asked which statement the author of the passage would agree with. In an excerpt from a fictional work, you might be asked to anticipate what the character would do next.

To answer such questions, you need to have a solid understanding of the topic and main idea of the passage. Armed with this information, you can figure out which of the answer choices best fits the criteria (or, alternatively, which do not). For example, if the author of the passage is advocating for safer working conditions in factories, any details that could be added to the passage should support that idea. You might select the answer choice that contains information about the number of accidents that occur in factories or that outline a new plan for fire safety.

SAMPLE QUESTION

Exercise is critical for healthy development in children. Today in the United States, there is an epidemic of poor childhood health; many of these children will face further illnesses in adulthood that are due to poor diet and lack of exercise now. This is a problem for all Americans, especially with the rising cost of health care.

It is vital that school systems and parents encourage children to engage in a minimum of thirty minutes of cardiovascular exercise each day, mildly increasing their heart rate for a sustained period. This is proven to decrease the likelihood of developmental diabetes, obesity, and a multitude of other health problems. Also, children need a proper diet, rich in fruits and vegetables, so they can develop physically and learn healthy eating habits early on.

6) **Which of the following statements might the author of this passage agree with?**
   A. Adults who do not have healthy eating habits should be forced to pay more for health care.
   B. Schools should be required by federal law to provide vegetables with every meal.
   C. Healthy eating habits can only be learned at home.
   D. Schools should encourage students to bring lunches from home.

FACTS VS. OPINIONS

In ParaPro reading passages you might be asked to identify a statement as either a fact or an opinion. A **fact** is a statement or thought that can be proven to be true. The statement *Wednesday comes after Tuesday* is a fact—you can point to a calendar to prove it. In contrast, an **opinion** is an assumption, not based in fact, that cannot be proven to be true. The assertion that *television is more entertaining than feature films* is an opinion—people will disagree on this, and there is no reference you can use to prove or disprove it.

QUICK REVIEW

Which of the following phrases would be associated with opinions?

for example, studies have shown, I believe, in fact, the best/worst, it's possible that

SAMPLE QUESTION

Exercise is critical for healthy development in children. Today in the United States, there is an epidemic of poor childhood health; many of these children will face further illnesses in adulthood that are due to poor diet and lack of exercise now. This is a problem for all Americans, especially with the rising cost of health care.

It is vital that school systems and parents encourage children to engage in a minimum of thirty minutes of cardiovascular exercise each day, mildly increasing their heart rate for a sustained period. This is proven to decrease the likelihood of developmental diabetes, obesity, and a multitude of other health problems. Also, children need a proper diet, rich in fruits and vegetables, so they can develop physically and learn healthy eating habits early on.

7) **Which of the following in the passage is a fact, not an opinion?**

A. Fruits and vegetables are the best way to help children be healthy.

B. Children today are lazier than they were in previous generations.

C. The risk of diabetes in children is reduced by physical activity.

D. Children should engage in thirty minutes of exercise a day.

SETS OF DIRECTIONS

The ParaPro requires you to understand and interpret directions. Some questions on the ParaPro may require you to follow a set of simple directions. These directions can be given in a paragraph format or list format. Usually, each step, or direction, includes specific instructions that must be remembered in order to complete the subsequent steps. The directions will require you to manipulate quantities (such as money or numbers of items) or shapes to reach the final answer.

HELPFUL HINT

Write out the new answer for each step as you finish it so you can easily check your work.

SAMPLE QUESTION

8) **You start with 3 red apples and 1 green apple in a basket. After following the directions below, how many apples are in the basket?**

1. **Remove 1 red apple.**
2. **Add 1 green apple.**
3. **Add 1 red apple.**
4. **Add 1 green apple.**
5. **Remove 2 red apples.**
6. **Remove 1 green apple.**
7. **Add 3 red apples.**
8. **Add 2 green apples.**

A. 4 red apples and 2 green apples
B. 4 red apples and 4 green apples
C. 2 red apples and 3 green apples
D. 0 red apples and 3 green apples

9) **You have 12 gallons of fuel in your tank. After following the directions below, how many gallons of fuel are left in the tank?**

1. **Use 1 gallon to drive to work.**
2. **Use 1 gallon to drive home.**
3. **Use 0.5 gallons to drive the kids to soccer practice.**
4. **Use 0.5 gallons to drive to the grocery store.**
5. **Use 2 gallons to drive back home.**

A. 2 gallons
B. 5.5 gallons
C. 7 gallons
D. 8.5 gallons

Printed Communications

On the ParaPro, you might be asked to interpret different types of text, and you will need to look at sources of information other than just a plain text passage. These sources may include invitations, advertisements, and memos. These **print communications** will include information presented both in text and graphic form. For example, an event flyer might have important information presented graphically, or you may need to look at the subject line of a memo to find its topic.

HELPFUL HINT

The strategies you learned for reading passages will help you answer questions about printed communications. For example, you might need to find the purpose of a memo or identify supporting details in an advertisement.

SAMPLE QUESTIONS

10) Which of the following are specific instructions given to the Human Resources Department?

A. Complete company business on personal computers during business hours.

B. Conduct standard monitoring of computer usage.

C. Communicate that personal use of computers is to occur only in emergency situations.

D. Communicate that personal computers should be limited to one hour per day.

11) What is the tone of this memo?

> MEMO
>
> To: Human Resources Department
>
> From: Corporate Management
>
> Date: December 6, 2013
>
> Subject: Personal Use of Computers
>
> The corporate office has been conducting standard monitoring of computer usage, and we have been quite dismayed at the amount of personal use occurring during business hours. Employee computers are available for the sole purpose of completing company business, nothing else. Personal use should occur only in emergency situations and should be limited to thirty minutes per day. Please communicate these requirements to lower management and personnel. These rules must be respected. If not, employees will be reprimanded by Management.

A. derisive

B. ambiguous

C. enraged

D. threatening

INDEXES AND TABLES OF CONTENTS

Paraprofessionals play a key role in helping students become readers and familiarizing them with text. Paraprofessionals may be asked to help students understand the parts of a book and so must be familiar with those parts themselves. An **index** is an alphabetical list of topics, and their associated page numbers, covered in a text. A **table of contents** is an outline of a text that includes topics, organized

> **QUICK REVIEW**
>
> When would it be appropriate to use an index but NOT a table of contents?

by page number. Both of these can be used to look up information, but they have slightly different purposes. An index helps the reader determine where in the text he or she can find specific details. A table of contents shows the reader the general arrangement of the text.

SAMPLE QUESTIONS

12) According to the index below, where might the reader find information about the nursing code of ethics?

A. pages 237 – 291
B. pages 189 – 296
C. pages 292 – 296
D. pages 189 – 236

13) A student has been assigned a set of homework questions from page 125. What topic will the questions cover?

Table of Contents

A. Pre-Algebra
B. Algebra
C. Geometry
D. Calculus

TEXT FEATURES

Text features are stylistic elements used to clarify, add meaning, or differentiate. Examples of text features include bold, italicized, or underlined fonts, and bulleted or numbered lists.

Bold fonts are generally used for emphasis. Italics should be used for titles of longer works, such as novels, movies, books, magazines, and plays. They are also used to denote a foreign word or phrase. Note that italicized fonts and underlined fonts serve similar purposes and are often used interchangeably. Underlining is more commonly used in handwritten documents.

SAMPLE QUESTION

14) Which of the following sentences properly uses italics?

A. We enjoyed our vacation in *Sacramento, California.*

B. Adam ate two plates of *pasta with meatballs.*

C. Angela's favorite book is *The Art of War.*

D. The traffic on *Main Street* is terrible during rush hour.

INTERPRETING VISUAL INFORMATION SOURCES

The ParaPro exam includes questions that test your comprehension of visual informational sources like graphs, diagrams, tables, and charts. You do not necessarily need to know about the topics covered in these sources; however you should feel comfortable looking at and understanding these types of sources.

GRAPHS AND CHARTS

Graphs and charts are used to present numerical data visually, in a way that is easy for the reader to understand. There are a number of different types of graphs and charts, each of which is useful for different types of data.

Bar graphs (also called **bar charts**) use bars of different lengths to compare amounts. The independent variable on a bar graph is grouped into categories such as months, flavors, or locations, and the dependent variable will be a quantity. Thus, comparing the lengths of the bars provides a visual guide to the relative quantities in each category.

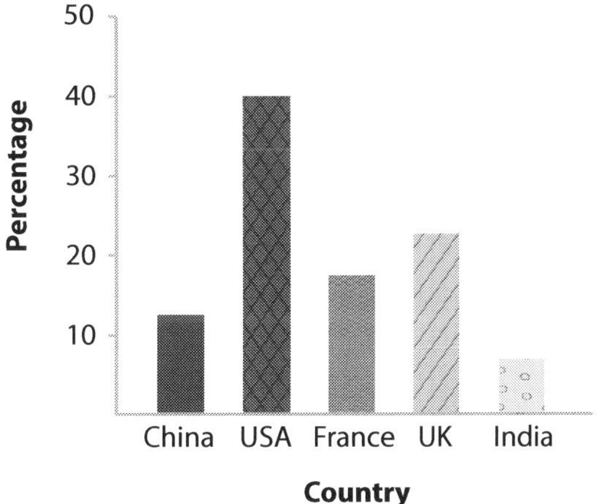

Figure 1.1. Bar Graph

Line graphs show changes in data by connecting points on a scatterplot using a line. These graphs will often measure time and are used to show trends in the data, such as temperature changes over a day or school attendance throughout the year.

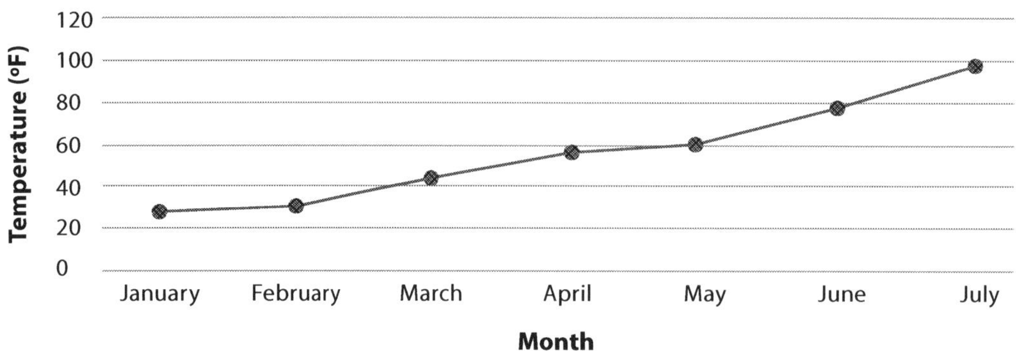

Figure 1.2. Line Graph

Pie charts (also called **circle graphs**) are used to show parts of a whole: the "pie" is the whole, and each "slice" represents a percentage or part of the whole.

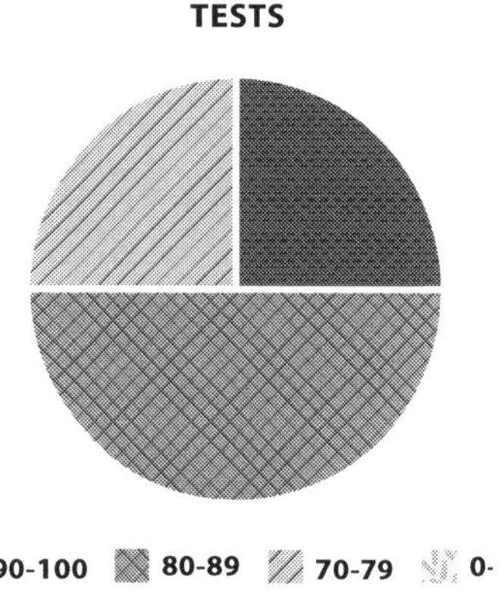

Figure 1.3. Pie Chart

SAMPLE QUESTIONS

Use the following pie chart for questions 15 and 16.

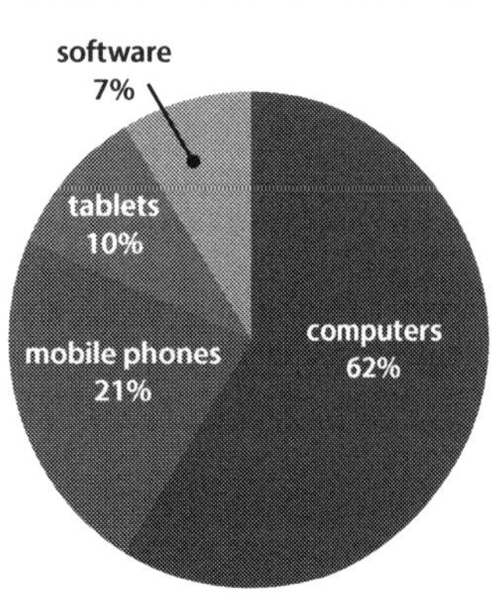

15) **Which of the following products accounts for the largest share of Wholesale Electronics' total sales?**

A. mobile phones

B. computers

C. software and tablets

D. software and mobile phones

16) **Mobile phones and tablets make up what percentage of Wholesale Electronics' total sales?**

A. 17 percent

B. 28 percent

C. 31 percent

D. 83 percent

TABLES

Tables display facts and concepts in a way that shows how they relate to each other. Tables are a very common visual aid; in fact, you have already seen some tables in this book.

Every table has a **title**, which explains what the table is about. Tables are composed of **cells** that contain information. Cells are laid out into rows and columns. **Rows**, read from left to right, show how information in the cells is related in one way. **Columns**, read from top to bottom, show how that information is related in another way. The columns have **headings**, which describe the types of information in the cells below. Rows may also have headings in some cases, which are usually located on the left-hand side of the page.

The table below is about types of educational support staff and their responsibilities. The rows show what the responsibilities are for a given job. Read another way, the columns describe the general educational support staff positions in schools and the duties undertaken by professionals in the educational environment.

Table 1.2. Educational Support Staff

Title	Duties
Paraprofessional	Trained teacher assistant who provides student support
Administrative assistant	Greets school visitors, answers phones, maintains organization for the office
Encumbrance clerk	Maintains financial responsibilities of the school
School nutritionist	Creates menu and oversees school nutrition program
Cafeteria staff	Provides nutritious meals and a sanitary environment for students

Table 1.2. Educational Support Staff (continued)

Title	Duties
Nurse	Provides general first aid, maintains health records of students, administers medication, provides health-related education
Custodian	Keeps the school building clean, may assist in other areas, such as moving furniture
Maintenance	Repairs electrical, heating, air, mechanical, and other issues that may affect the physical operation of a school building
Computer technician	Provides service and maintenance of computer-related equipment
Bus driver	Provides safe transportation to and from school and to school-related activities

SAMPLE QUESTION

Use the example below to answer question 17.

Faculty	
Title	**Duties**
Teacher	Teaches students in a specialized grade or content area using approved curriculum; maintains relationships with students, parents, and colleagues
Counselor	Provides social skills training and academic counseling; frequently creates class schedules and serves as the testing coordinator
Special education teacher	Teaches students who have been identified with a disability; writes and implements individualized education plan (IEP) with the help of IEP team
Library/media specialist	Oversees operation of the school library, teaches library and research skills, supports teachers in obtaining resources

17) According to the table above, how do the duties of a special education teacher differ from the duties of other teachers?

A. Special education teachers teach students who have been identified with a disability.

B. Special education teachers do not write or implement IEPs with the help of an IEP team.

C. There is no difference; both types of teachers teach all students at the school.

D. Special education teachers support other teachers in obtaining resources.

DIAGRAMS

A **diagram** is a visual representation of an object or scene. Individual elements or parts of the object or scene are labelled. Diagrams are especially important in science.

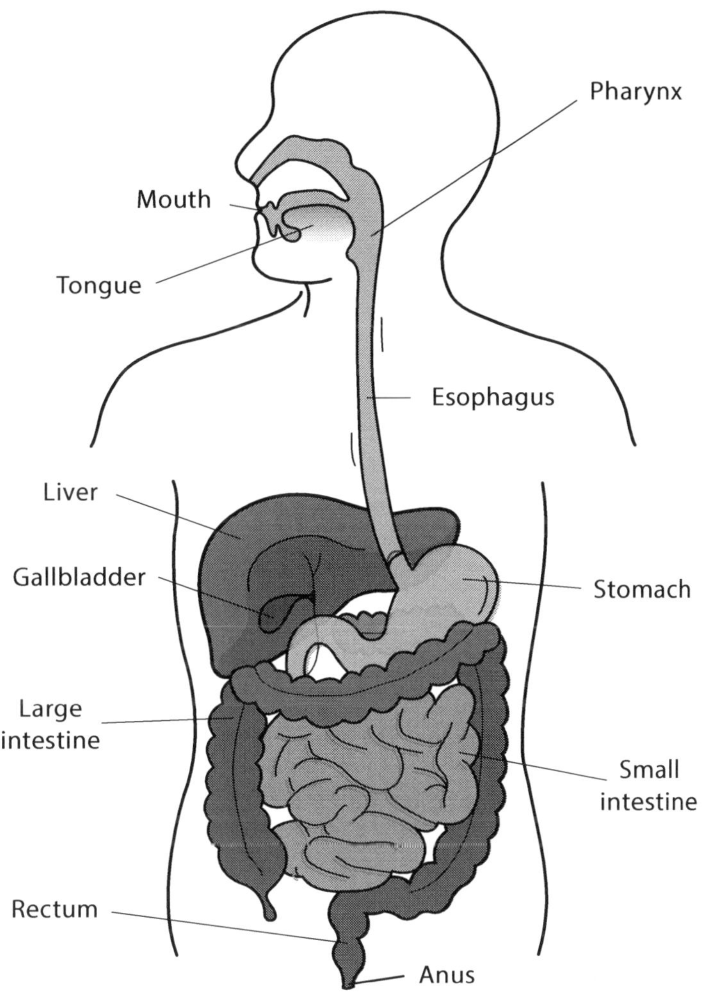

Figure 1.4. Diagram: The Digestive Tract

SAMPLE QUESTION

18) **In the diagram of the digestive tract above, what organ is located directly above the anus?**

   A. liver

   B. esophagus

   C. tongue

   D. rectum

Answer Key

1. **D.** **Correct.** Choice A can be eliminated because it directly contradicts the rest of the passage. Choices B and C can also be eliminated because they offer only specific details from the passage. While both choices contain details from the passage, neither is general enough to encompass the passage as a whole. Only choice D provides an assertion that is both backed up by the passage's content and general enough to cover the entire passage.

2) **B.** **Correct.** Choice B is the first sentence of the passage and introduces the topic. Choice A is the final sentence of the passage and summarizes the passage's content. Choices C and D are supporting sentences found within the body of the passage. They include important details that support the main idea of the passage.

3) **A.** **Correct.** The passage states, "The topography of Venus, for example, has been explored by several space probes, including the Russian Venera landers and NASA's *Magellan* orbiter." The other choices are mentioned in the passage, but are not space probes.

4) **B.** **Correct.** Choice B is the best option because it addresses the use of multiple technologies to study the surface of planets. Choices C and D can be eliminated because they do not address the topic of studying the surface of planets. Choice A can also be eliminated because it only addresses a single technology.

5. **C.** **Correct.** The passage starts by introducing the topic of candidate quotas, then goes on to explain how these quotas have affected the number of female legislators and CEOs. The transition *as a result* links the cause to the effect.

6) **B.** **Correct.** Since the author argues that children need *a proper diet, rich in fruits and vegetables*, we can infer that the author would agree with choice B. The author describes the cost of health care as a problem for all Americans, implying that he would not want to punish adults who never learned healthy eating habits (choice A). Choices C and D are contradicted by the author's focus on creating healthy habits in schools.

7) **C.** **Correct.** Choice C is a simple fact stated by the author. It is introduced by the word *proven* to indicate that it is supported by evidence. Choice B can be discarded immediately because it is not discussed anywhere in the passage, and also because it is negative, usually a hint in multiple-choice questions that an answer choice is wrong. Choices A and D are both opinions—the author is promoting exercise, fruits, and vegetables as a way to make children healthy. (Notice that these incorrect answers contain words that hint at being an opinion such as *best or should.*)

8) B. **Correct.** Starting with 3 red apples and 1 green apple, and following the directions, you have:

1. 2 red apples and 1 green apple
2. 2 red apples and 2 green apples
3. 3 red apples and 2 green apples
4. 3 red apples and 3 green apples
5. 1 red apple and 3 green apples
6. 1 red apple and 2 green apples
7. 4 red apples and 2 green apples
8. 4 red apples and 4 green apples

9) C. **Correct.** Starting with 12 gallons, and following the directions, you have:

1. 11 gallons after driving to work.
2. 10 gallons after driving home from work.
3. 9.5 gallons after driving the kids to soccer practice.
4. 9 gallons after driving to the grocery store.
5. 7 gallons after driving back home.

10) C. **Correct.** According to the memo, the Human Resources Department is to communicate to lower management and personnel that personal use of company computers is to occur only in emergency situations.

11) D. **Correct.** The memo threatens that *employees will be reprimanded* if the given rules are not followed.

12) A. **Correct.** According to the index, this information can be found between pages 237 and 291.

13) C. **Correct.** According to the table of contents, page 125 is in Chapter 3: Geometry.

14) C. **Correct.** The sentence in choice C italicizes the title of a longer work and is therefore correct. Italics are not used for names of cities (choice A), foods (choice B), or streets (choice D).

15) B. **Correct.** Computers account for 62 percent of sales. Mobile phones (choice A) are 21 percent, software and tablets (choice C) equal 17 percent, and software and mobile phones (choice D) equal 28 percent.

16) C. **Correct.** Mobile phones (21 percent) and tablets (10 percent) together account for 31 percent of Wholesale Electronics' total sales.

17) A. **Correct.** According to the table, special education teachers teach students who have been identified with a disability; they also write and implement IEPs with the help of an IEP team.

B. Incorrect. Under *Duties*, it clearly states that special education teachers are responsible for writing and implementing IEPs with the help of an IEP team.

C. Incorrect. According to the table, only special education teachers are responsible for teaching those students who have been identified with a disability.

D. Incorrect. The table states that library/media specialists are responsible for supporting teachers in obtaining resources, listing that task under *Duties* for that title.

18) A. Incorrect. Many organs appear between the anus and the liver.

B. Incorrect. The esophagus is located well above the anus on the diagram.

C. Incorrect. According to the diagram, the tongue is far above the anus.

D. **Correct.** On the diagram, the rectum is shown immediately above the anus.

Application of Reading Skills and Knowledge to Classroom Instruction

On the ParaPro, questions will present you with classroom situations about reading-related tasks. Paraprofessionals should know about the **foundations of reading**. The foundations of reading concern what students need to know when they learn the basics of words and written text. The ParaPro will test your ability to help students sound out words, break down words into their parts, use context clues, understand synonyms, antonyms, and homonyms, and alphabetize words.

Questions will also ask about the **tools of the reading process**. These tools are specific classroom strategies to help students improve their reading skills. Questions will assess your ability to assist students in prereading strategies, which include skimming the text and making predictions about it. Test questions may also address assisting students in using a dictionary, asking students about a passage to help them understand it better, interpreting directions, and making observations about students' reading abilities.

Foundational Skills of Reading

Phonemic Awareness

At the early literacy stage, teachers provide opportunities for students to internalize the link between oral and written language with exercises that reinforce phonological awareness. Such exercises also introduce students to the **alphabetic principle**, or the way that sounds and letters work together to create a decipherable code for giving and receiving messages. Understanding the alphabetic principle means understanding that certain letters signify certain sounds. Teachers utilize rhyming books, books with repetitive text, engaging poems, play, and music to focus student attention on the sound units, or phonemes, that make up words. A selection of developmentally appropriate strategies follows; these reinforce phonological awareness and introduce the alphabetic principle.

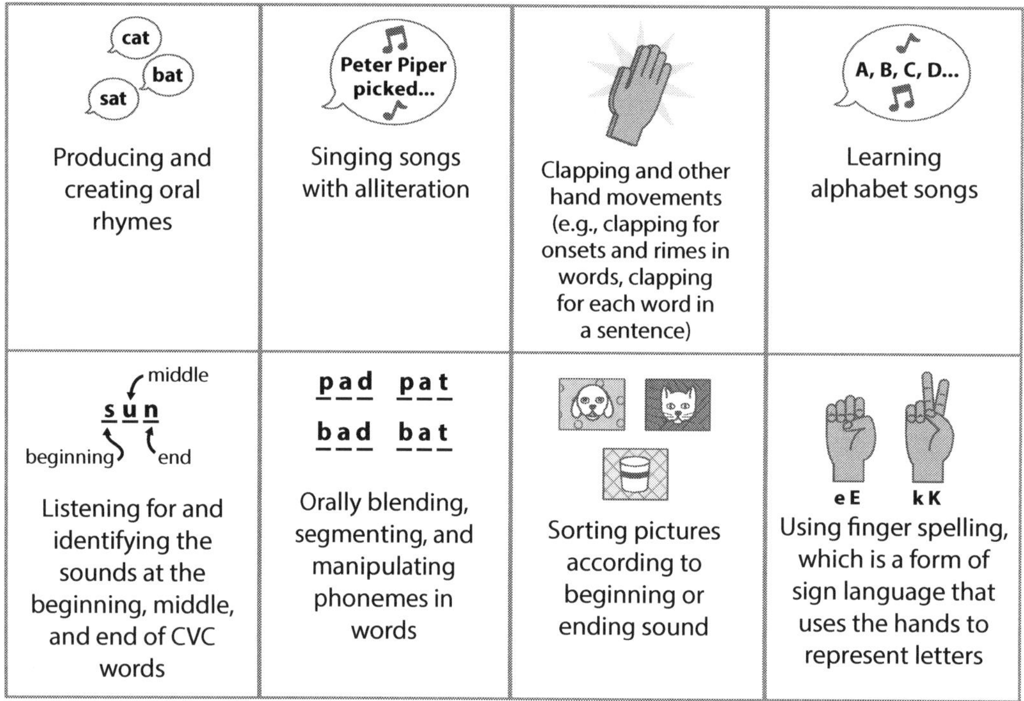

Figure 2.1. Phonological Awareness Strategies

Phonological awareness is an understanding of how sounds, syllables, words, and word parts can be orally manipulated to break apart words, make new words, and create rhymes. It is an important foundational skill for learning to read and literacy development. **Phonemic awareness** is a type of phonological awareness that focuses on the sounds in a language. It is an understanding of how each small unit of sound, or **phoneme**, forms the language by creating differences in the meanings of words. For example, the phonemes /m/ and /s/ determine the difference in meaning between the words *mat* and *sat*.

There are forty-four different phonemes in the English language. These include letter combinations such as consonant diagraphs like /sh/ and vowel diphthongs like /oy/ where the letters work together to produce one sound. Teachers build phonemic awareness in their students using a variety of techniques such as phoneme blending, phoneme segmentation, phoneme substitution, and phoneme deletion.

Table 2.1 Phoneme Chart

Phoneme	Example	Phoneme	Example	Phoneme	Example
Consonants		***Vowels***		***R-controlled vowels***	
/b/	Bat	/a/	Lap	/ă/	Hair
/d/	Dog	/ā/	Late	/ä/	Art
/f/	Fish	/e/	Bet	/û/	Dirt
/g/	Goat	/ē/	See	/ô/	Draw

Phoneme	Example	Phoneme	Example	Phoneme	Example
Consonants		***Vowels***		***R-controlled vowels***	
/h/	Hat	/i/	Hit	/ēə/	Rear
/j/	Jump	/ī/	Ride	/üə/	Sure
/k/	Kick	/o/	Hop	**Digraphs**	
/l/	Laugh	/ō/	Rope	/zh/	Measure
/m/	Milk	/oo/	Look	/ch/	Chick
/n/	No	/u/	Cut	/sh/	Shout
/p/	Pot	/ū/	Cute	/th/	Think
/r/	Rat	/y//ü/	You	/ng	Bring
/s/	Sit	/oi/	Oil		
/t/	Toss	/ow/	How		
/v/	Vote	/ə/ (schwa)	Syringe		
/w/	Walk				
/y/	Yak				
/z/	Zoo				

Phoneme blending is combining phonemes to make a word; for example, /m/ /a/ /t/ combine to form *mat*. In contrast, **phoneme substitution** is the replacement of phonemes in words to make new words; removing the /m/ from the beginning of the word *mat* and replacing it with /s/ creates the word *sat*. **Phoneme segmentation** is separating phonemes in words; separating the sounds in the word *mat* isolates the phonemes /m/ /a/ /t/. Finally, in **phoneme deletion**, phonemes are removed from words to make new words. Removing /m/ from *mat* leaves the word *at*.

Building phonemic awareness in students is the latter part of a developmental sequence that contributes to a strong foundation in phonological awareness. Prior to focusing on phonemic awareness, teachers build phonological awareness with exercises that task students with orally manipulating the phonological units of spoken **syllables**. These phonological units are defined as onsets and rimes and can be blended, substituted, segmented, and deleted just like phonemes. The **onset** of a syllable is the beginning consonant or consonant blend. The **rime** includes the syllable's vowel and its remaining consonants. For example, in the word *block*, the consonant blend /bl/ is the onset, and the remainder of the word *–ock* is the rime.

QUICK REVIEW

A teacher reads students the following series of words: ball, call, fall, mall, tall. What phonemic awareness strategy is this teacher using?

SAMPLE QUESTION

1) **A paraprofessional says *hat* and instructs a student to produce the sounds she hears in the word. Which strategy is the paraprofessional using to build phoneme awareness?**

A. phoneme blending

B. phoneme deletion

C. phoneme segmentation

D. phoneme substitution

Phonics and Word Recognition

Once students have a solid foundation in phonological awareness, they are ready to begin phonics instruction. **Phonics** is the study of the relationship between the spoken sounds in words and the printed letters that correspond to those sounds, or **letter-sound correspondence**. Beginning with one-to-one letter-sound correspondences, teachers focus students on making connections between letter sounds and printed letters. This is followed by teaching techniques for **decoding** text (pronouncing written words based on knowledge of letter-sound relationships) such as word pattern recognition and blending and segmenting sounds in printed words.

Initial lessons focus on sounding out and manipulating the letters in names, signs, and labels, and progress from there. Teachers complement phonics instruction with word study activities to establish a foundational reading vocabulary of recognizable words, including high-frequency words and sight words. Teachers use a variety of strategies and approaches to implement phonics and word study lessons, some of which are shown in the figure below.

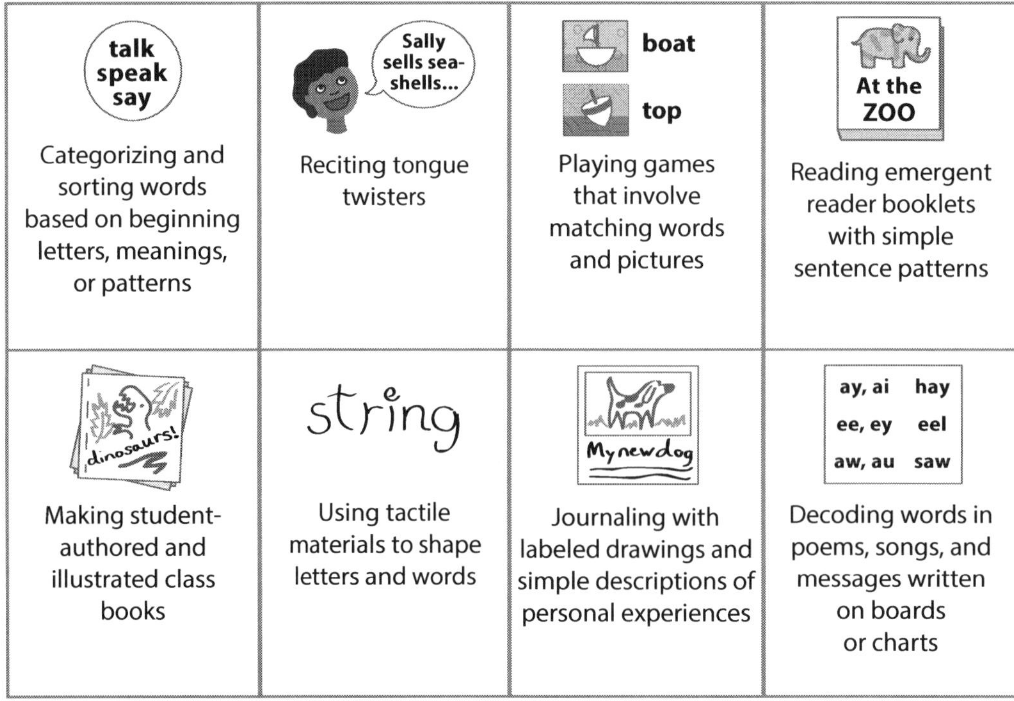

Figure 2.2. Phonics Strategies

Initially, the most common sounds for each letter and **high frequency** letter-sound correspondences, or those that occur most often in the English language, are introduced. In order to assist students beginning to read simple VC (vowel-consonant), VCC (vowel-consonant-consonant), CVCC (consonant-vowel-consonant-consonant), and CVC (consonant-vowel-consonant) words early on, a few short vowel sounds are introduced as well. Letters with names that bear a strong relationship to their sounds are introduced before letters that do not. For example, the sound of the letter *s* can be heard at the end of its name.

Phonics instruction progresses from simple to more complex letter-sound correspondences and sound/spellings (or the spelling of words based on letter-sound correspondences). Short-vowel sound spellings are introduced before long-vowel sound/spellings, and letters that are similar in appearance (e.g., *b* and *d*) or sound (e.g., /m/ and /n/) are taught separately along the instructional continuum. As students move through kindergarten and the primary grades, they progress from decoding two- or three-phoneme words with letters representing their most common sounds to longer words and more complex sound/spelling patterns.

Sight words, words that are repeated most often in text, are taught in conjunction with phonics. These are words that students need to learn to recognize by sight, such as *a*, *in*, *the*, *at*, and *I*, in order to read sentences with optimal fluency. As with letter-sound correspondences and sound/spellings, sight word instruction begins with the most common words, or highest frequency words. Teachers develop sight word lists for students using either the *Dolch List of Basic Sight Words* or *Fry's Numerical List of Instant Words*. These lists change and evolve across grade levels so that students build a large repertoire of instantly recognizable words as they move through the primary grades.

READING COMPREHENSION

Fluency, or the ability to automatically recognize words in print and recite them in a fluid, expressive manner, is critical to **reading comprehension**, or the ability to make meaning from text. For this reason, paraprofessionals model reading at an appropriate rate with accuracy and meaningful expression when working with students. In order to help students learn how reading with fluency sounds and feels, paraprofessionals may engage in repeated readings of familiar picture books with patterns, rhymes, and engaging illustrations. They encourage students to read with them, or **choral read**, during the predictable parts of books or while following along in copies of the book, reciting each word in unison.

Guided reading is another technique paraprofessionals use to model the behaviors of readers who read for meaning. During guided reading, paraprofessionals pause during reading to ask questions about the words, pictures, characters, events, and information encountered in text in order to maximize understanding of content. The paraprofessional may ask students to identify and pronounce words, make predictions, analyze character behaviors, use pictures as clues to meaning, and make inferences. Students should also practice restating information in their own words and make connections to themselves, other books, and the outside world. As students transition to independent readers, guided reading is used to monitor progress in small groups as students take turns reading aloud. **Repeated reading**, or reading the same section of text over and over until errors are eliminated, is used to increase fluency. Educators ask open-ended questions about the text to gauge students' level of comprehension.

Finally, **concepts of print** familiarize students with the structures and purposes of books and other reading materials. Students learn that books have a front cover, a back cover, an author, and often an illustrator. They learn that letters, words, and sentences convey messages to readers about different topics, both real and imaginary. They gain an understanding of how books are read from top to bottom, left to right, one line after the next. Students become familiar with **text layout**—text size, text organization in paragraphs or columns, and the presence of illustrations—as educators and paraprofessionals display and read various texts aloud, allowing students to follow along. They model appropriate reading behaviors, which students practice by looking through books independently, both individually and in small groups. A selection of developmentally appropriate strategies that reinforce print concepts is presented below.

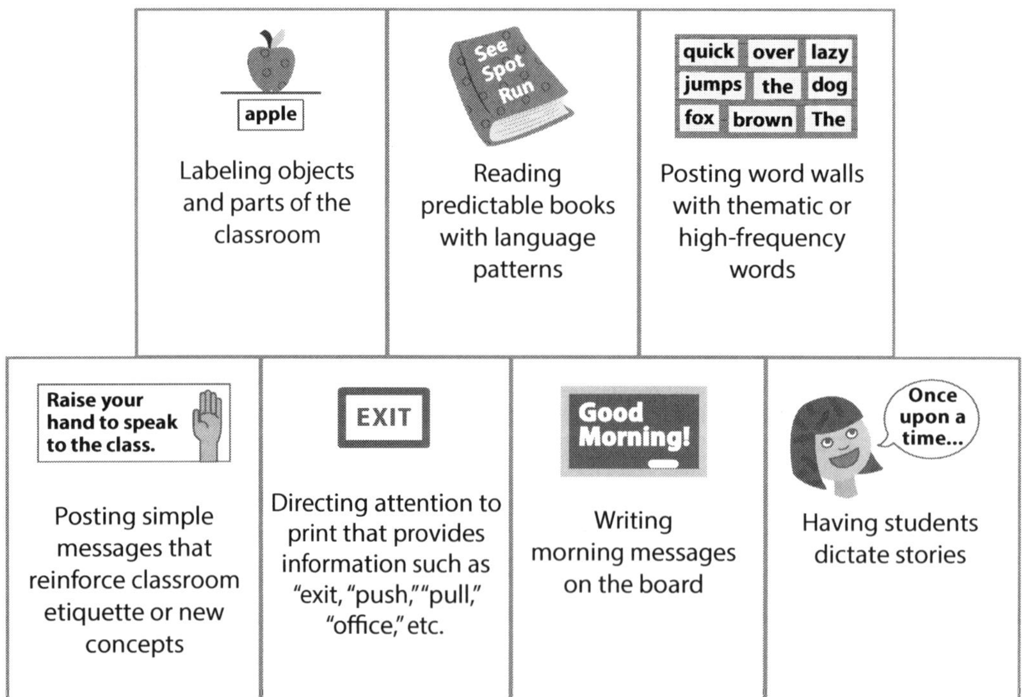

Figure 2.3. Strategies to Reinforce Concepts of Print

SAMPLE QUESTION

2) **Mr. Falls is reading aloud from a predictable picture book. He has written a refrain from the story on a sentence strip that is displayed on a pocket chart. Each time the refrain occurs in the story, Mr. Falls signals his students to read aloud with him as he points to each word. Which of the following is Mr. Falls demonstrating?**

   A. decoding

   B. predicting

   C. concepts of print

   D. word analysis

THE READING PROCESS

A student becomes a reader when he or she is able to describe and analyze the content being read. Language arts teachers **scaffold** reading comprehension strategies so that students can progress toward independent reading proficiency at developmentally appropriate levels with tasks that challenge without overwhelming. Teachers break reading tasks into manageable chunks and provide students with tools and strategies for mastering each chunk.

Because students enter classrooms at a variety of reading levels, teachers must be able to assess a diverse set of reading needs and differentiate lessons accordingly for both struggling and advanced readers. Paraprofessionals play a key role in the classroom by providing extra support when students vary in levels of reading ability.

The tools and strategies employed in an optimal reading comprehension curriculum provide pathways for students to **think critically** (actively and explicitly conceptualize, apply, analyze, synthesize, and/or evaluate information to form a conclusion) in order to interpret the purposes and meanings of written text across a variety of genres and styles. Exercises in reading comprehension take place before, during, and after reading.

Before reading, during **prereading**, teachers have students make observations, connections, and predictions related to book titles, cover illustrations, text features, and background knowledge. They activate prior knowledge and pre-teach new vocabulary. To generate interest, teachers may choose literature (fiction and nonfiction in story form) and informational text (academic nonfiction) that relates to themes or topics that students are learning about in other subject areas. By connecting text to student experience, teachers can build on what is already known about a topic and increase understanding by challenging students to interpret new information.

During reading, paraprofessionals monitor understanding by pausing to ask questions about characters, setting, theme, figures of speech, vocabulary, main ideas, supporting details, points of view, plot development, and text organization. They also ask questions that require students to make inferences related to dialogue, behavior, word choice, and the author's intentions. In so doing, paraprofessionals model **thinking aloud**, or verbalizing thoughts and insights, so that students learn to pause and reflect during reading to maximize and facilitate comprehension. **Graphics** such as maps, tables, photographs, and graphs, can be provided and analyzed to clarify difficult academic concepts, historical eras, or author motivations.

HELPFUL HINT

When reading a book or article with pictures, pause to ask students to discuss what is happening in the picture before reading the relevant section. This will give students context for the reading that follows.

After reading, students have the opportunity to summarize text and draw conclusions about the author's message. Students participate in activities in which they consider new text in relation to other materials on the same topic (print and multimedia) in order to make informed judgments about personal, local, and global subjects and situations. Students are also provided opportunities to participate in creative and collaborative activities (e.g., writing, art, reader's theater, field trips, research, or debate) that reinforce comprehension and extend learning.

Key Ideas and Details

Readers must use key ideas and details from literary or informational text to determine the moral, theme, or central idea; make inferences; and summarize information. Readers must also be able to analyze characters, setting, plot, and relationships among ideas, events, and concepts. Paraprofessionals help students learn these skills.

The **theme** of a literary text is the basic idea that the author wants to convey. It weaves in and out of the text as the story, play, or poem unfolds. It expresses an underlying opinion related to the text's subject. On the other hand, the **moral** of a literary text is the lesson the author wants to teach the reader. It is more direct than a theme. The basic underlying idea of informational text is referred to as the **central idea**. This is the major focus of the information provided in the text.

QUICK REVIEW

Consider the familiar story of "The Tortoise and the Hare." What is the central idea of the story? What is the theme of the story? How do they differ?

The goal of teaching reading comprehension is not just to have students arrive at conclusions, but to come to *evidence-based* conclusions. Accordingly, students are urged to formulate responses to and interpretations of the texts they read; then, they must cite specific **details** or **evidence** to support their conclusions. In the early grades, students begin by referring to the text when looking for answers to questions provided in class. When they get older, they move to asking their own questions and quoting text to articulate their answers. By middle school, they should be able to cite details in the text in order to explain and justify their thinking.

In addition to using evidence themselves, students must also be able to identify and interpret an author's use of evidence in the context of an informational text. They must learn how to evaluate arguments based on the evidence and claims made in support of those arguments. One of the most efficient ways of having students evaluate the reliability of an article is to have them explore how well the writer supported his or her ideas. In the classroom, a teacher might have students first identify the claims of an article, then look for the evidence the writer includes to substantiate the claim. Evidence can then be evaluated based on its source. The paraprofessional would assist students in identifying the evidence in the text and its sources, for example.

Students should be aware that, even in informational texts, they will have to draw their own inferences to fully make sense of what they are reading. Readers draw **inferences** when they use their own knowledge in combination with details from the text to understand the meaning of a sentence, paragraph, or passage.

Summarization is the distillation and condensation of a text into its main idea and key details. It is a short encapsulation of what the text is about and clarifies the general message. To properly summarize fictional texts, it is important to identify **story elements**. These elements include the characters (e.g., main, minor, protagonist, antagonist, dynamic, static), **setting** (where the story takes place), and **plot** development (e.g., exposition, rising action, problem/climax, falling action, resolution) in a text. Understanding the role of a character in a story via the character's actions, traits, relationship, and personality is **character analysis**. Analyzing how a character thinks and behaves allows a reader to understand the character's motivations and beliefs.

Summarization is an important skill for students to improve their reading comprehension; it also helps the paraprofessional gauge whether a student fully understands a reading selection.

SAMPLE QUESTION

3) What is an inference based on?

A. facts and specific examples in the text

B. textual details and the reader's own knowledge

C. understanding the author's purpose

D. recognizing the author's tone

Author's Craft and Text Structure

Authors have numerous tools at their disposal. They can choose between words with similar meanings, organize text in many different ways, or change a story's point of view. These choices together define the author's craft, or the techniques authors use to tell stories or build arguments in a text.

Authors consider a number of factors when selecting words. First, they consider both the denotation and the connotation of a word. The **denotation** of a word is its meaning, the meaning that can be found in the dictionary. The **connotation** of a word, on the other hand, is its suggested or implied meaning. Connotation can be positive or negative, based on the emotional associations of the word.

Word choice helps build the **tone** of a literary work, which is created by the author's attitude toward the reader and toward the subject of the text. In a sense, it is the tone of voice used to speak to the reader. Depending on word choice, an author's tone can range anywhere from playful and familiar to alarmed and forceful. Students should be encouraged to consider how the author uses language to communicate tone and what the author is suggesting through word choice. Often, this line of questioning will reveal the author's attitude and, ultimately, the theme of the work.

Texts are built by starting with smaller parts that are added together to create meaning. In a fiction or informational text, words are combined to form **sentences**, which can in turn be combined to build **paragraphs**. In longer texts, paragraphs can be further grouped into **chapters**.

In poetry, words combine to form **lines**, which are separated by some sort of punctuation, meter, and/or rhyme. Lines are grouped together to form **stanzas**, units of lines that are typically arranged in a pattern created by meter and/or a rhyme scheme.

In a play, the dialogue and stage directions work together to create a distinct **scene**, which typically takes place in a single location and is often defined by the changing of characters on the stage. Scenes are grouped together into **acts**. Many plays follow a traditional three- or five-act structure.

Analyzing text organization is the ability to analyze the way a text is organized in order to better comprehend an author's purpose for writing. Authors choose the organizational structure of their text according to their purpose; for example, an author who hopes to convince people to begin recycling might begin by talking about the problems that are caused by excessive waste and end by offering recycling as a reasonable solution. Different **text structures** include:

- **Cause and effect**: shows a causal chain of events or ideas, with each event connected to or leading to another
- **Problem and solution**: begins with examining the details of something and concludes by offering a possible solution to the issue

- **Sequential order**: arranges events in the order in which they occur, either in consecutive or logical order
- **Chronological order**: presents events in the order in which they occurred in time
- **Compare and contrast**: highlights the similarities and differences between multiple items or ideas

> QUICK REVIEW
>
> Consider how word choice heightens the impact of Dr. Martin Luther King Jr.'s famous "I Have a Dream" speech. What connotation does the word *dream* have in this context? Why would he choose that word over other options like *wish* or *plan*?

Some texts offer supplemental information outside of the main text. These **text features** include imagery like photographs, drawings, maps, charts, and graphs, many of which may include captions that describe or add context to the figures. Text features also include organizational features like chapter headings, titles, and sidebars (boxes of explanatory or additional information set aside from main text) as well as **tables of contents** and **indices**. Students should be able to use these features to expand their understanding of the text and to quickly locate relevant information.

An author uses a specific point of view to tell a story. When identifying **point of view**, readers use genre and pronoun clues to identify who is telling a story to best form accurate conclusions about the events of the story. Typically, authors use one of five points of view: first-person, second-person, third-person objective, third-person limited omniscient, and third-person omniscient. In **first-person** point of view, one character tells the story from their direct experience using pronouns such as *I*, *my*, *mine*, and *we*. In **second-person** point of view, the perspective of the text is from an external "you," whether that be the reader or unknown other.

In **third-person objective** point of view, a detached narrator relates the actions and dialogue of the story, but not the thoughts or feelings of any characters. In **third-person limited omniscient** point of view, a detached narrator tells the story from one character's point of view including that character's internal thoughts and feelings. In **third-person omniscient** point of view, a detached and all-knowing narrator tells the story from the point of view of all of the characters, including all of their thoughts and feelings. Any text told from a third-person point of view includes pronouns such as *he*, *she*, *it*, and *they*.

SAMPLE QUESTIONS

4) What tool should a paraprofessional help students use to find content related to a specific word or idea in a book?

A. table of contents

B. footnotes

C. chapter titles

D. index

5) **Read the following text:**

The day started out quite normally when my alarm clock rang. I got out of bed, flipped on the bathroom light, and stumbled to the sink. I brushed my teeth in a daze and then got dressed. Moving to the kitchen, I poured my coffee and headed for the door. Just then, a loud BANG rang out, and everything went dark.

What type of text structure is used in this passage?

A. cause and effect

B. problem and solution

C. sequential order

D. compare and contrast

Text Types

Literature can be classified into **genres**, categories of works that are similar in format, content, tone, or length. Most works fall into one of four broad genres: nonfiction, fiction, drama, and poetry.

Nonfiction is a genre of prose writing defined by the use of information that is, to the best of the author's knowledge, true and accurate. Nonfiction texts are written to inform, to reflect, and to entertain. **Fiction** is a prose genre, made up of narratives whose details are not based in truth but are instead the creation of the author. Fiction is typically written in the form of novels and short stories.

Drama is expressive writing that tells a story to an audience through the actions and dialogue of characters, which are brought to life by actors who play the roles onstage. Dramatic works, called **plays**, can be written in poetic or lyrical verse or in regular prose. Along with the **dialogue** between the characters, authors rely on **stage directions** to describe the sets and to give directions to the actors about what they are to do.

Poetry is imaginative, expressive verse writing characterized by rhythm, unified and concentrated thought, concrete images, specialized language, and use of patterns. Different poetic forms utilize techniques and structures in unique ways.

Text can also be classified based on the author's purpose for writing. There are four main writing **styles** that students learn in elementary school:

- **Expository writing**: This style of writing is primarily used to explain an idea or concept or inform the reader about a topic. It is most often used in formal essays that include a main idea and supporting details based on fact.
- **Narrative writing**: This style of writing is primarily used to tell a personal or fictional story that entertains the reader. The author includes descriptive details and figurative language in order to maintain the reader's attention with dynamic characters, interesting settings, and

captivating plots. Poems that tell stories, or **narrative poems**, also use this writing style.

- **Descriptive writing**: This style of writing emphasizes the production of imagery using words and figurative language that appeal to the reader's five senses. It is a writing style that produces vivid pictures in the reader's imagination and is often used to write poetry or detailed descriptions of experiences or events.
- **Persuasive writing**: This style of writing is used to convince, or persuade, a reader to subscribe to the author's opinion or point of view. It follows a formal progression that aims to sway the reader into accepting the author's stance and often plays on the reader's emotions to achieve its goal. Persuasive writing is often used for **speeches** and **advertisements**.

SAMPLE QUESTION

6) **Which of the following can be classified as persuasive writing?**

   A. an advertisement for a new product

   B. a research paper on the effects of climate on ecosystems

   C. a poem about the ocean on a foggy day

   D. a short story with a suspenseful plot

GRAPHIC ORGANIZERS

Charts and graphic organizers are used as tools to support students as they draw meaning from content. **Graphic organizers** provide ways of organizing ideas and information in order to clarify thinking. Some of the main types of reading comprehension graphic organizers are listed below:

- **KWL Chart**: This is a three-column chart with the headings *K*, *W*, and *L*. The first column lists what students already *know* (K) about a topic, the second column lists what students *want* (W) to know about a topic, and the third column lists what students *learned* (L) from reading about the topic.
- **Venn Diagram**: This is a diagram that is used to compare and contrast texts that treat similar stories or topics in different ways. For example, a teacher may read the same fairy tale told by two different authors. Students could then use Venn diagrams to organize the similarities and differences of the two stories.
- **Sequencing Chart**: This organizer is used by students to correctly order the events in a story or the steps in a procedure. Students either arrange picture cards or sentences, or draw pictures and write sentences.
- **Main Idea/Key Detail Chart**: This chart is an organizational aid for recording the main idea of an informational text and the key details

that support the main idea. Prior to using the organizer, students learn how to search introductory and concluding paragraphs for main ideas and body paragraphs for supporting details.

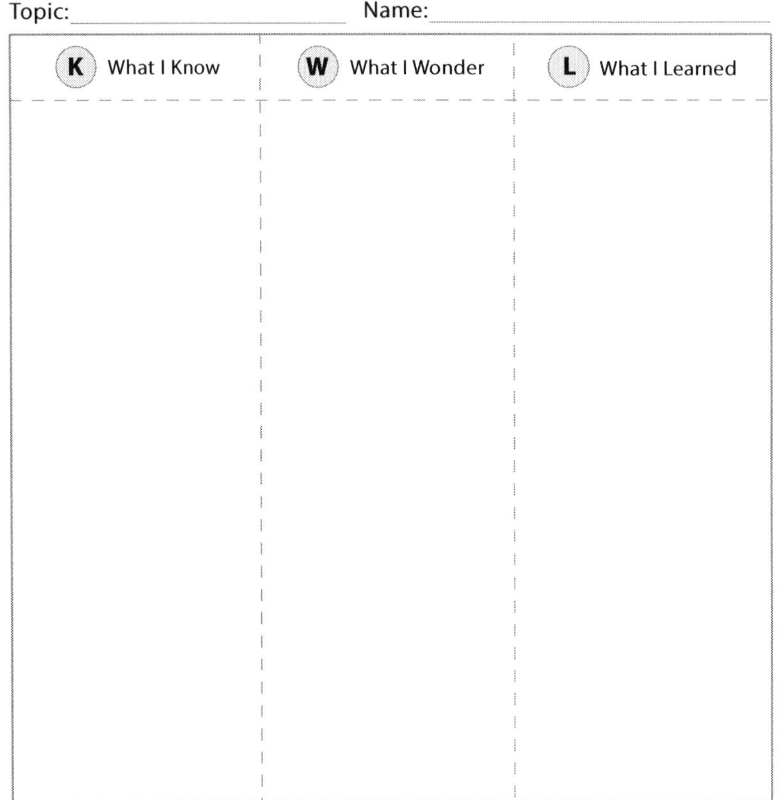

Figure 2.4. KWL Chart

- **Fact and Opinion Chart**: This organizer provides columns where students construct lists of facts and opinions encountered in text. Students learn that facts are truths proven with hard evidence, while opinions are thoughts or beliefs that are unproven. Students learn to look for numerical clues to determine facts and word clues such as *believe* and *should* to determine opinions. In later grades, student use their knowledge of facts and opinions to identify **reasoned judgments**, or points of view supported by reasons and evidence.
- **Problem and Solution Diagram**: This diagram is an organizational aid for recording the central problem in a story and the events that lead to its resolution.
- **Plot Pyramid**: This visual is an organizational aid for identifying the plot development in a story. With an understanding of the characteristics of exposition, rising action, climax, falling action, and resolution, students can delve deeper into an author's reasons for using particular events, dialogue, and literary devices to move a story forward.

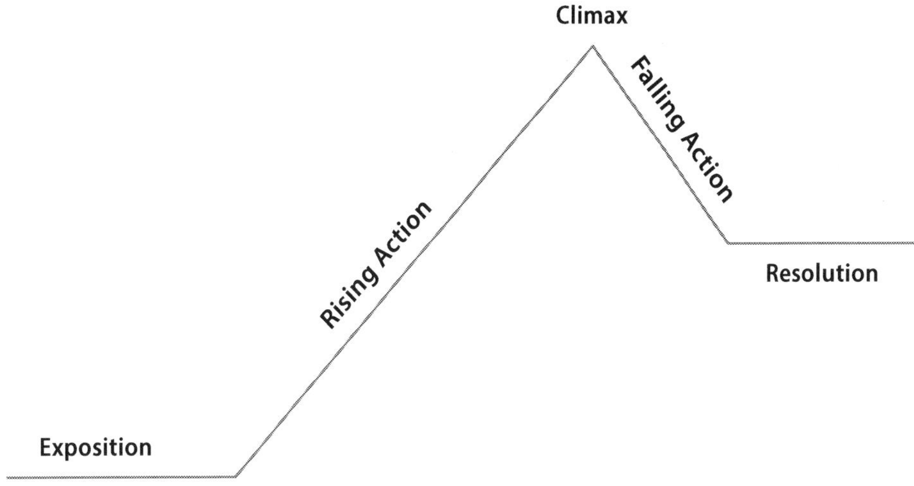

Figure 2.5. Plot Pyramid

- **Text Structure Chart**: This is a tool that prompts students to identify the relationships between ideas in a text and the signal words that reveal those relationships. Signal words provide clues to the structure an author is using to present information. For example, a sequencing text structure will include signal words such as *first*, *next*, and *last*; a cause-and-effect structure will include signal words and terms such as *consequently*, *as a result*, and *in order to*.

Education professionals assist students in creating these tools to help them better understand the texts they read.

SAMPLE QUESTIONS

7) **Before students begin a new literature book, Ms. Bean introduces them to a list of vocabulary words from the book and has them work in groups to develop skits that demonstrate the meaning of each word. Which of the following is Ms. Bean demonstrating?**

   A. thinking aloud
   B. scaffolding
   C. identification of signal words
   D. informed judgment

8) **A paraprofessional notices that a student who has just finished reading a novel is having difficulty identifying how the story transitions from one stage to another. Which of the following is the best graphic organizer to help the student understand the story's development?**

   A. a plot pyramid
   B. a Venn diagram
   C. a main idea/key details chart
   D. a sequencing chart

Integration and Application of Knowledge

Once a student can decode a text and determine its meaning, the student must then be able to apply that knowledge. Students should be able to evaluate the argument presented by the author in a text. This includes identifying the author's reasoning and the evidence supporting it, and then determining the sufficiency, relevance, and quality of that reasoning.

For students to do this effectively, teachers must guide them in assessing sources. Students must also understand basic logical reasoning. Teachers should ask students to explain the relationships between evidence and argument. For example, when reading an informational text, teachers can ask students to identify the main idea of a particular section and then point to details in the section that support that main idea.

Teachers should also provide students the opportunity to practice developing their own arguments and reasoning supported by source-based evidence. In the early grades, this involves simple writing assignments, primarily based on personal opinion and experience. As students develop, they should be able to address a broader range of topics and draw on a variety of high-quality academic sources. Similarly, by middle school, students should be able to critique a wide variety of academic writing.

In addition to evaluating evidence, students must learn how to integrate information across multiple texts. This integration can take several different forms. Information from multiple sources can be **synthesized** to create a fuller understanding of a concept. In synthesis, specific details about a topic are taken from multiple sources and layered. For example, a student researching frogs might read an encyclopedia entry, a *National Geographic* article, and a poem. Each source provides different information that the student then brings together to create a unified understanding of frogs.

Secondly, information from different sources can also be *compared* to determine similarities and differences in the approach, style, and ideas of different authors. To do this effectively, students must be able to identify both the purpose and bias of authors.

Finally, students should be able to *analyze* the format of different sources to understand how different forms lead to different tones and meaning in a text. This includes evaluating the role that illustrations and visual representations play in the reader's understanding of a text. For example, in an early grade classroom, the teacher might read a book aloud to the class in which the visuals provide information beyond the text of the book. The teacher would then encourage students to discuss what the images convey and how that information relates to the text.

Application of knowledge from a text also involves extrapolating information from one source and applying it to new sources, new contexts, and new ideas. As students develop, they should be able to use existing knowledge to make sense of new texts, and then to apply the knowledge learned to other new ideas or problems.

The teacher can aid the student in developing this skill by using the charts and graphic organizers discussed earlier. The curriculum should also include a repetition of knowledge and skills in different contexts to aid students in making connections among concepts.

SAMPLE QUESTIONS

9) **A student is studying mammals. After learning about characteristics of whales, the student hypothesizes about the characteristics of hippos. What is the student demonstrating?**

A. The student is synthesizing information.

B. The student is applying knowledge to a new context.

C. The student is comparing ideas and concepts.

D. The student is analyzing the format of a text.

10) **Which of the following activities would best help students evaluate an author's argument?**

A. drawing a Venn diagram

B. create a diagram of the claim and evidence

C. examining a second source at a lower reading level

D. writing a short essay summarizing the argument

VOCABULARY

Learning new vocabulary is an essential experience in reading. Paraprofessionals assist students by helping them use context clues, analyze word structure, and understand synonyms, antonyms, and homonyms.

CONTEXT CLUES

Questions on the ParaPro ask examinees to prove their ability to help students use **context clues** to learn new vocabulary. The paraprofessional is expected to assist students in taking sentences apart to identify these clues. Questions may present situations and ask about possible solutions to help the student arrive at the correct answer.

Restatement clues state the definition of the word in the sentence. The definition is often set apart from the rest of the sentence by a comma, parentheses, or a colon.

Paraprofessionals should understand the basics of cognition, the ability to apply new information to other settings and to draw conclusions.

The meaning of *cognition* is restated following the comma as "the ability to apply new information to other settings and to draw conclusions."

Contrast clues include the opposite meaning of a word. Words like *but*, *on the other hand*, and *however* are tip-offs that a sentence contains a contrast clue.

> The teacher wanted to offer remediation to the struggling student, but the school lacked the required supplementary resources.

> *Remediation* is contrasted with "required supplementary resources," so the definition of remediation is "additional support."

Positive/negative clues tell you whether a word has a positive or negative meaning.

> The paraprofessional suggested offering enrichment to the student who had quickly mastered the required curriculum.

> The positive descriptions *quickly* and *mastered* suggest that *enrichment* has a positive meaning.

SAMPLE QUESTIONS

11) Henry is struggling with the meaning of *achievement* in this sentence:

The student was proud of his achievement: he had completed an important project and earned an "A."

How can the paraprofessional help Henry decode the meaning of the word *achievement* using context clues?

A. Tell Henry to look up *achievement* in a dictionary.

B. Help Henry identify positive and restatement clues.

C. Explain to Henry what positive and restatement clues are.

D. Suggest Henry look for words like *but*, *however*, or *despite*.

Select the answer that most closely matches the definition of the underlined word or phrase as it is used in the sentence.

12) The dog was dauntless in the face of danger, braving the fire to save the girl trapped inside the building.

A. difficult

B. fearless

C. imaginative

D. startled

13) Beth did not spend any time preparing for the test, but Tyrone kept a rigorous study schedule.

A. strict

B. loose

C. boring

D. strange

WORD ANALYSIS AND WORD STRUCTURE

Paraprofessionals help students break complex words down into their main parts to help determine their meaning and build vocabulary. These activities are called **word analysis** exercises. This component of reading instruction is also known as **morphology**, or how the forms and structures of words contribute to their meanings.

Most words can be broken down into **affixes** (**prefixes** and **suffixes**) and **roots**, which teaches students how word parts provide clues to the meanings of whole words and their functions in sentences. Attaching prefixes and suffixes to roots *morphs*, or changes, the meanings of words. As students learn more affixes, they can build vocabulary.

> **HELPFUL HINT**
>
> The word *affix* means to attach. *Affixes* are units of letters that attach to either the beginning or the end of a word.

prefix - root - suffix

Roots are the building blocks of all words. Every word is either a root itself or has a root. The root is what is left when you strip away the prefixes and suffixes from a word. For example, in the word *unclear*, if you take away the prefix *un–*, you have the root *clear*.

Roots are not always recognizable words, because they often come from Latin or Greek words, such as *nat*, a Latin root meaning born. The word *native*, which means a person born in a referenced place, comes from this root; so does the word *prenatal*, meaning *before birth*. It is important to keep in mind, however, that roots do not always match the original definitions of words, and they can have several different spellings.

Prefixes are elements added to the beginning of a word, and **suffixes** are elements added to the end of the word; together they are known as **affixes**. They carry assigned meanings and can be attached to a word to completely change the word's meaning or to enhance the word's original meaning.

Let's use the word *prefix* itself as an example: *fix* means to place something securely and *pre–* means before. Therefore, *prefix* means to place something before or in front of. Now let's look at a suffix: in the word *morphology*, *morph* is a root which means change. The suffix *–ology* means study. Thus, *morphology* is the study of change—here, how the meanings of words change when affixes are added to roots.

Although you cannot determine the meaning of a word from a prefix or suffix alone, you can use this knowledge to eliminate answer choices. Understanding whether the word is positive or negative can give you the partial meaning of the word.

Table 2.2. Common Roots and Affixes

Root	Definition	Example
ast(er)	star	asteroid, astronomy
audi	hear	audience, audible
auto	self	automatic, autograph
bene	good	beneficent, benign
bio	life	biology, biorhythm
cap	take	capture
ced	yield	secede
chrono	time	chronometer, chronic
corp	body	corporeal
crac or crat	rule	autocrat
demo	people	democracy
dict	say	dictionary, dictation
duc	lead or make	ductile, produce
gen	give birth	generation, genetics
geo	earth	geography, geometry
grad	step	graduate
graph	write	graphical, autograph
ject	throw	eject
jur or jus	law	justice, jurisdiction
juven	young	juvenile
log or logue	thought	logic, logarithm
luc	light	lucidity
man	hand	manual
mand	order	remand
mis	send	transmission
mono	one	monotone
omni	all	omnivore
path	feel	sympathy
phil	love	philanthropy
phon	sound	phonograph
port	carry	export
qui	rest	quiet
scrib or script	write	scribe, transcript
sense or sent	feel	sentiment

Root	Definition	Example
tele	far away	telephone
terr	earth	terrace
uni	single	unicode
vac	empty	vacant
vid or vis	see	video, vision

Table 2.3. Common Prefixes

Prefix	Definition	Example
a– (also an–)	not, without; to, toward; of, completely	atheist, anemic, aside, aback, anew, abashed
ante–	before, preceding	antecedent, anteroom
anti–	opposing, against	antibiotic, anticlimax
belli–	warlike, combative	belligerent, antebellum
com– (also co–, col–, con–, cor–)	with, jointly, completely	combat, cooperate, collide, confide, correspond
dis– (also di–)	negation, removal	disadvantage, disbar
en– (also em–)	put into or on; bring into the condition of; intensify	engulf, embrace
hypo–	under	hypoglycemic, hypodermic
in– (also il–, im–, ir–)	not, without; in, into, toward, inside	infertile, impossible, illegal, irregular, influence, include
intra–	inside, within	intravenous, intrapersonal
out–	surpassing, exceeding; external, away from	outperform, outdoor
over–	excessively, completely; upper, outer, over, above	overconfident, overcast
pre–	before	precondition, preadolescent, prelude
re–	again	reapply, remake
semi–	half, partly	semicircle, semiconscious
syn– (also sym–)	in union, acting together	synthesis, symbiotic
trans–	across, beyond	transdermal
trans–	into a different state	translate
under–	beneath, below; not enough	underarm, undersecretary, underdeveloped

On the ParaPro, examinees are tested on their ability to help students break down words into their parts and to help them learn new words from those parts. Students study affixes and roots and draw on their knowledge of other words to build their vocabularies.

SAMPLE QUESTIONS

14) Tanisha has asked for help determining the meaning of the word *unfavorable*. How can the paraprofessional help Tanisha decode the meaning of this word using word analysis?

A. Ask Tanisha to identify any familiar prefixes, suffixes, and roots.

B. Remind Tanisha to study her lists of roots and affixes.

C. Give Tanisha the meanings of the affixes so that she can understand the word.

D. Tell Tanisha to look up the root of the word, *favor*, in the dictionary.

15) Which of the following concepts involves understanding how the forms and structures of words contribute to their meanings?

A. phonology

B. mechanics

C. paraphrasing

D. morphology

Select the answer that most closely matches the definition of the underlined word or phrase as it is used in the sentence.

16) The <u>bellicose</u> dog will be sent to training school next week.

A. misbehaved

B. friendly

C. scared

D. aggressive

17) The new menu <u>rejuvenated</u> the restaurant and made it one of the most popular spots in town.

A. established

B. invigorated

C. improved

D. motivated

Analyzing Words

Determining the meaning of a word can be more complicated than just looking in a dictionary. A word might have more than one **denotation**, or definition, and which one the author intends can only be judged by looking at the surrounding text. For example, the word *quack* can refer to the sound a duck makes or to a person who publicly pretends to have a qualification which he or she does not actually possess.

A word may also have different **connotations**, which are the implied meanings and emotions a word evokes in the reader. For example, a cubicle is simply a walled desk in an office, but for many the word implies a constrictive, uninspiring workplace. Connotations can vary greatly between cultures and even between individuals.

Last, authors might make use of **figurative language**, which is the use of a word to imply something other than the word's literal definition. This is often done by comparing two things. If you say *I felt like a butterfly when I got a new haircut*, the listener knows you do not resemble an insect but instead felt beautiful and transformed.

SAMPLE QUESTIONS

Select the answer that most closely matches the definition of the underlined word or phrase as it is used in the sentence.

18) The patient's uneven pupils suggested that brain damage was possible.

- **A.** part of the eye
- **B.** student in a classroom
- **C.** walking pace
- **D.** breathing sounds

19) Aiden examined the antique lamp and worried that he had been taken for a ride. He had paid a lot for the vintage lamp, but it looked like it was worthless.

- **A.** transported
- **B.** forgotten
- **C.** deceived
- **D.** hindered

SYNONYMS, ANTONYMS, AND HOMONYMS

Paraprofessionals must help students identify and differentiate among synonyms, antonyms, and homonyms. **Synonyms** are words that can stand in for each other. For instance, *car* and *automobile* are synonyms: they are interchangeable and mean the same thing. Words that mean the opposite of each other are **antonyms**. *Hot* and *cold* are antonyms: they are opposites.

Table 2.4. Common Synonyms

answer	solution
asked	questioned
brave	courageous

Table 2.4. Common Synonyms (continued)	
cat	feline
delicious	tasty
dog	hound
easy	simple
fast	quick
focus	concentrate
friend	pal
giant	massive
huge	enormous
important	significant
junk	trash
kind	considerate
love	affection
multiply	increase
nice	pleasant
opportunity	chance
perfect	flawless
regular	ordinary
smart	intelligent
thankful	grateful
unhappy	sad
very	extremely
walk	stroll
worried	nervous
yellow	blond
zero	nil

Table 2.5. Common Antonyms	
angry	calm
beautiful	ugly
coward	hero
different	similar
educated	ignorant
fearful	brave

generous	selfish
happy	sad
interested	bored
jagged	smooth
lies	truth
lift	drop
microscopic	enormous
nice	unpleasant
open	closed
probable	unlikely
question	answer
respect	contempt
silence	noise
trusting	wary
under	over
vigorous	lazy
wide	narrow
willing	reluctant
yank	extend
zigzag	straight line

Homonyms are slightly more complex. There are two types of homonyms. **Homographs** are words that are spelled and pronounced the same way, but have different meanings. They can only be differentiated in context. For instance, *duck* is a homograph: A *duck* is a bird that can swim and fly; a person might *duck* to avoid a projectile (such as a flying duck!). **Homophones** are words that are spelled differently but pronounced the same way, with different meanings. In their written form, it is easy to tell them apart, but when spoken aloud they are only distinguished by context. *Poll* and *pole* are homophones. A person might swing from a *pole*, or take a *poll* of opinions on a given topic.

Table 2.6. Common Homonyms

address (a physical location)	address (to speak directly to someone)	
affect (to change something)	effect (the result of an action)	
bear (a large, carnivorous mammal)	bear (to carry a weight or burden)	bare (to be without any cover, such as clothing or other protection)

Table 2.6. Common Homonyms (continued)		
can (a metal container that preserves food)	can (a verb describing the ability to do an action: *I can…*)	
cent (one hundredth of a dollar)	scent (a smell)	sent (to have been dispatched)
down (going below or under a given location)	down (a soft covering)	
days (units of time measured in twenty-four hours)	daze (a stunned state of being)	
exact (precise)	exact (to take something)	
earn (to accumulate deserved payment or compensation, usually for work)	urn (a container)	
found (discovered)	found (to establish)	
fairy (a mythological creature)	ferry (a vehicle that transports people between two or more locations)	
general (typical)	general (a military leader)	
gait (a speed of walking or running)	gate (a portal in a fence or wall)	
hide (to keep from being discovered by someone or something)	hide (skin, leather)	
heel (the back of the foot)	heal (to ease pain or disease)	
isle (island)	aisle (a row or passageway)	
just (fair)	just (exactly)	
jewel (a precious stone)	joule (unit of measure for energy)	
kind (type)	kind (nice)	
knead (to squeeze and press something to make it soft, such as dough)	need (to require)	
lie (to be dishonest)	lie (to recline)	
leak (when liquid accidentally escapes its container)	leek (a type of vegetable)	
match (a contest or game)	match (a device used to start a fire)	

made (to have been constructed or completed)	maid (a worker who assists in domestic duties)	
nail (a thin fastener with a head, usually pounded with a hammer)	nail (a keratin growth extending from fingers and toes)	
night (the period of time between sunset and sunrise)	knight (a warrior during medieval times in Europe)	
object (an item)	object (to have an opposing opinion, to refuse)	
oar (a device used to propel boats)	ore (minerals)	or (a conjunction used to denote an alternative, often between two or more people, places, things, or concepts)
park (a public location for recreation, usually featuring greenery)	park (to stop a car and position it to be turned off and abandoned, temporarily or permanently)	
pail (bucket)	pale (light colored, sickly)	
quarry (an area where minerals are harvested)	quarry (prey, game)	
quartz (a type of mineral)	quarts (plural of *quart*, the measurement of one-fourth of a gallon)	
right (correct)	right (opposite of *left*)	
racket (noise)	racquet (a device used to play tennis)	
saw (the past tense of the verb *to see*)	saw (a device used for cutting wood, metal, and other tough materials)	
sail (a device used on boats to harness wind, aiding in propulsion)	sale (the selling of goods and services, providing a discount)	
tear (a rip in fabric or other material)	tear (a salty liquid released by the tear glands near the eyes when crying)	
tale (a story)	tail (a body part located at the posterior of many animals)	
utter (to say, to mutter)	utter (total, complete)	udder (organ on a cow that produces milk)

Table 2.6. Common Homonyms (continued)		
vain (self-absorbed)	vain (fruitless, pointless, to do something *in vain*)	vein (a vessel that transports blood in the body)
vary (to change)	very (really)	
watch (to observe)	watch (a device that attaches to the wrist and tells time)	
wail (to cry out)	whale (a large aquatic mammal)	
yard (a unit of measurement spanning three feet)	yard (an enclosed outdoor area)	
yoke (harness)	yolk (part of an egg)	

The ParaPro tests examinees on their ability to help students navigate synonyms, antonyms, and homonyms. For students to understand these words, they should be able to identify them and understand the surrounding context of the reading selection. The role of the paraprofessional is to help students identify synonyms, antonyms, and homonyms in the text. The paraprofessional also helps students focus on the broader context of a reading selection so that they can make sense of problematic words, especially homonyms. To better understand context, paraprofessionals read aloud with students. Choral reading, guided reading, and repeated reading are key, in addition to helping students study specific antonyms, homonyms, and synonyms.

SAMPLE QUESTIONS

Select the best word for the blank in the following sentences.

20) Our school's ____ will decide whether Aaron will be expelled.

A. principle

B. principal

C. students

D. teachers

21) What word is most closely a synonym for the word *chaotic*?

A. dangerous

B. uncaring

C. haphazard

D. harmonious

ANSWER KEY

1) A. Incorrect. The strategy of phoneme blending requires the student to combine phonemes to make a word.

B. Incorrect. The strategy of phoneme deletion requires the student to remove phonemes in words to make new words.

C. **Correct.** The strategy of phoneme segmentation requires the student to separate the phonemes in a word.

D. Incorrect. The strategy of phoneme substitution requires the student to replace phonemes in words to make new words.

2) A. Incorrect. In decoding, Mr. Falls would model how to pronounce words using knowledge of letter-sound relationships.

B. Incorrect. To demonstrate predicting, Mr. Falls would pause to ask students what they think might happen next in the story's plot development.

C. **Correct.** By having students listen to predictable text and chant the refrain with him as he points to individual words, Mr. Falls is reinforcing concepts of print, clarifying that words and letters convey meaning, words are constructed of letters, and text is read from left to right.

D. Incorrect. Mr. Falls is not demonstrating word analysis because he is not asking students to break apart words into roots and affixes in order to determine the words' meanings.

3) A. Incorrect. It is true that readers use details of the text to infer meaning. However, an inference is made when certain information is not explicitly stated and readers have to fill in the blank.

B. **Correct.** In order to read between the lines, readers must use their own knowledge as well as draw on the information provided.

C. Incorrect. Understanding the author's purpose may help a reader to draw an inference, but it is not necessarily essential to the process.

D. Incorrect. Readers can infer an author's tone, but tone itself does not necessarily provide enough information for one to make an inference.

4) A. Incorrect. The table of contents helps readers identify specific chapters or general topics.

B. Incorrect. Footnotes provide information on sources referenced in the text or offer clarification and further details on subject matter.

C. Incorrect. Chapter titles indicate the general subject of a specific chapter, not the exact terms covered.

D. **Correct.** An index allows the reader to find the location of specific words or concepts in a text.

5) A. Incorrect. The text does not explain how one event led to another.

B. Incorrect. The text does not introduce a problem or offer a resolution to one.

C. Correct. The text explains events in the order in which they occurred in the story.

D. Incorrect. The text does not address similarities and differences between ideas or things.

6) A. Correct. Persuasive writing aims to influence the reader to agree with what is stated and to act accordingly. The purpose of an advertisement is to convince the reader to buy a product.

B. Incorrect. A research paper is an example of expository writing and is often neutral in tone.

C. Incorrect. A poem using sensory imagery is an example of descriptive writing.

D. Incorrect. A short story with a plot arc is an example of narrative writing.

7) A. Incorrect. Thinking aloud is when a teacher verbalizes thoughts and insights to model pausing and reflecting during reading to maximize and facilitate comprehension.

B. Correct. Ms. Bean is scaffolding instruction by pre-teaching difficult vocabulary so that meanings are easily accessed during reading. In this way, she can focus student attention on another reading comprehension strategy (beyond vocabulary development) during reading.

C. Incorrect. The identification of signal words is a reading comprehension strategy related to text structure.

D. Incorrect. Students are prompted to make informed judgments on a topic after the topic has been thoroughly investigated via different materials and sources.

8) A. Correct. A plot pyramid helps students identify and visualize how an author moves a story forward in clear stages with specific characteristics: exposition, rising action, climax, falling action, and resolution.

B. Incorrect. A Venn diagram is used to organize the similarities and differences between two texts.

C. Incorrect. Students would use a main idea/key details chart to identify the main idea of an informational text and the most significant details supporting that idea.

D. Incorrect. A sequencing chart helps students order events in a story, but it does not task them with identifying how the events work together to move the story forward as elements of plot structure.

9) A. Incorrect. Synthesizing is integrating information from different sources.

B. Correct. Whales and hippos are both mammals, so the student is using the former to understand the latter.

C. Incorrect. The number of texts the student is working with is not discussed.

D. Incorrect. The student is examining content, not format.

10) A. Incorrect. A Venn diagram helps a reader compare the similarities and differences between two arguments or issues, not evaluate the strength of an argument.

B. Correct. The strength of an author's argument is in the connection between claim and evidence.

C. Incorrect. While studying another, more elementary source may help some students understand the context better, it will not help them to evaluate the argument.

D. Incorrect. Writing a summary may help a student better understand a text, but it does not necessarily improve a student's evaluation of the author's argument.

11) A. Incorrect. Henry does not need a dictionary to determine the meaning of *achievement* in this sentence; he can use context clues.

B. Correct. This sentence contains positive clues: the modifiers *proud* and *important*, as well as the high grade of A. It also has a restatement clue, the clause "he had completed an important project and earned an 'A.'"

C. Incorrect. Rather than explaining the concepts behind positive and restatement clues, it would be more helpful for the paraprofessional to help Henry deconstruct the actual sentence to make sense of the words.

D. Incorrect. Words like *but*, *however*, and *despite* are useful when determining the meaning of words using contrast clues, but no contrast clues appear in this sentence. Therefore, this technique is not useful in helping Henry figure out the meaning of the word *achievement*.

12) B. Correct. Demonstrating bravery in the face of danger would be *fearless*. The restatement clue (*braving*) tells you exactly what the word means.

13) A. Correct. The word *but* tells us that Tyrone studied in a different way than Beth, which means it is a contrast clue. If Beth did not study hard, then Tyrone did. The best answer, therefore, is choice A.

14) A. Correct. The paraprofessional can assist Tanisha in separating roots and affixes. In the word *unfavorable*, there are two common affixes: the prefix *un–* and the suffix *–able*, modifying the root word *favor*. The paraprofessional could suggest Tanisha search the word for familiar roots and affixes to deduce the meaning of the word.

B. Incorrect. It is useful for students to study vocabulary, including roots and affixes, but the paraprofessional can provide more support to Tanisha in this situation.

C. Incorrect. Telling Tanisha what most of the word means—even just the affixes—robs her of the chance to learn. Tanisha may already know what the affixes mean and just need a reminder to search for them in the word. The paraprofessional should guide her in analyzing the word, not analyze it for her.

D. Incorrect. The paraprofessional should begin by helping Tanisha analyze the word herself. If Tanisha still does not know the meaning of the root, *favor*, then it might be useful to advise her to use a dictionary, but that should not be the first step.

15) A. Incorrect. Phonology focuses on the relationships between the oral sounds that make up a language.

B. Incorrect. Mechanics is concerned with the conventions of print, such as punctuation, that are used to provide pacing and expression cues in written text.

C. Incorrect. Paraphrasing is the ability to restate a spoken or written message in one's own words.

D. Correct. Morphology investigates how the forms and structures of words contribute to their meanings.

16. D. Correct. Both misbehaved and aggressive look like possible answers given the context of the sentence. **However, the prefix** *belli–*, **which means warlike, can be used to confirm that aggressive is the right answer.**

17) B. Correct. All the answer choices could make sense in the context of the sentence, so it is necessary to use word structure to find the definition. The root *juven* means young and the prefix *re–* means again, so *rejuvenate* means to be made young again. The answer choice with the most similar meaning is *invigorated*, which means to give something energy.

18) A. Correct. Only choice A matches both the definition of the word and context of the sentence. Choice B is an alternative definition for pupil, but does not make sense in the sentence. Both C and D could be correct in the context of the sentence, but neither is a definition of pupil.

19) C. Correct. It is clear from the context of the sentence that Aiden was not literally taken for a ride. Instead, this phrase is an example of figurative language. From context clues you can figure out that Aiden paid too much for the lamp, so he was deceived.

20) B. Correct. The *principal* is the administrative head of a school; a *principle* is a strongly held belief. *Students* and *teachers* would be grammatically correct, but *principal* fits the context of the sentence better.

21) C. Correct. *Haphazard* means "a lack of planning or order." For example, when a room is arranged haphazardly, it is disorganized, messy, and chaotic.

Mathematics

Counting and Operations with Whole Numbers

Counting

Numeracy concepts provide children with the mathematical foundation they need so that they can use math in their everyday lives. Children must have a clear understanding of numeracy concepts before they can begin to understand and apply more difficult concepts such as place value, addition, and subtraction. Children must become familiar and comfortable with numbers, their roles, and their relationships. For example, they need to understand what the number 2 is, how to show that number using objects, and the role of the number 2 in other processes (such as describing quantities).

Students start by memorizing number sequences (1, 2, 3, and so on) and learning to recite sequences of whole numbers. They can then begin to learn **one-to-one correspondence**, connecting a single number to a single object and learning to count objects. Once this skill is mastered, they can be introduced to the concept of **cardinality**, or the number of items in a set. As students become comfortable counting objects in a set, they should be able to **subitize**, or accuractly recognize small quantities quickly without explicitly counting the objects.

> HELPFUL HINT
>
> Connect counting to cardinality: When counting objects in a set, the last word said is the number of objects in that set.

The main key in teaching numeracy concepts is the use of **manipulatives**. Instruction should include a variety of concrete activities using various manipulatives in order for children to gain a clear understanding of these concepts. Some examples of manipulatives that can be used include unifix cubes, Dienes blocks, beans, beads, popsicle sticks, coins, buttons, playing cards, sorting mats, number/coin stamps, dominoes, and five/ten frames (just to name a few).

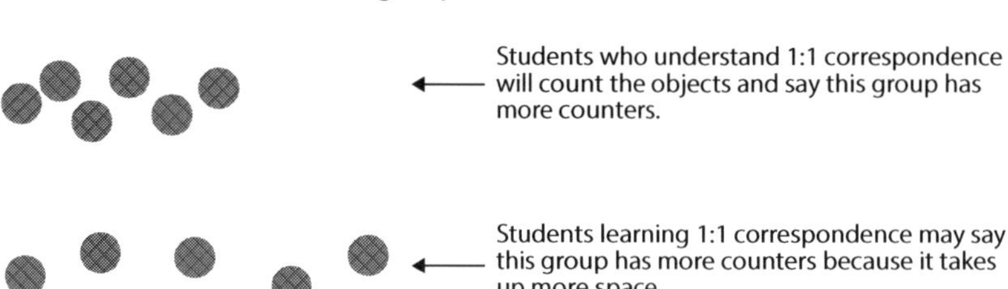

Figure 3.1. One-to-One Correspondence

Children need to engage in a variety of hands-on activities that allow the exploration of numbers. The objective of these activities is to make children comfortable with numbers, what they mean, and the role they play in the environment.

SAMPLE QUESTIONS

1) **Which activity is most appropriate for a student who is learning to count to ten?**

   A. comparing integers on a number line

   B. drawing pictures of combinations that equal ten

   C. matching the numeral ten to cards with ten items on them

   D. counting, comparing, and sorting ten plastic bears

2) **A first-grade teacher provides students a part/part/whole mat and cubes. The teacher asks the students to find a way to make the number 7 using the cubes and mat. The teacher is most likely helping the students to understand**

   A. the different number pairs that will equal the number 7.

   B. how to identify the number of items in a set.

   C. how to show conservation of numbers.

   D. how to compare numbers.

Number Theory

A basic foundation in number theory is vital for understanding more advanced mathematical concepts. Students begin working with **natural numbers**, which are used when counting (e.g., 1, 2, 3, etc.). Once a basic understanding of natural numbers is achieved, more advanced concepts, such as whole numbers and integers, can be introduced. **Whole numbers** are similar to natural numbers, except that whole numbers include zero. **Integers** are positive or negative whole numbers (not fractions or decimals).

Rational numbers are numbers that can be made by dividing two integers. Rational numbers must be expressed as a terminating or a repeating decimal, such as 0.125 or $0.\overline{66}$. **Irrational numbers** have a decimal part that does not terminate or repeat. Pi (π) is an example of an irrational number ($\pi = 3.14159265...$). Integers are rational numbers because they can be written as a fraction with a denominator of 1.

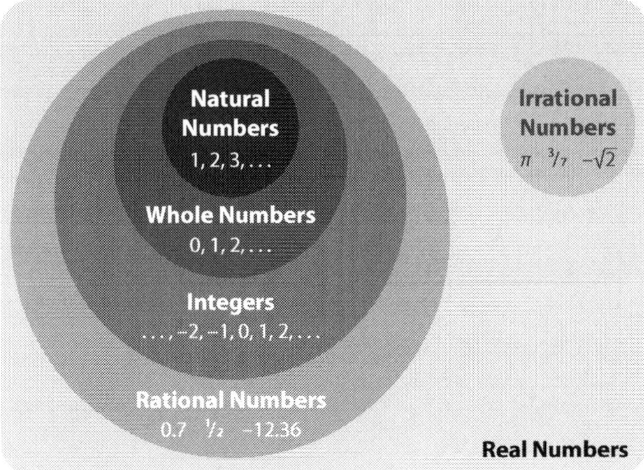

Figure 3.2. Types of Numbers

The set of rational and irrational numbers make up the set of **real numbers**. Real numbers can be represented on a **number line**, where 0 is in the middle, positive numbers are to the right, and negative numbers are to the left. Figure 3.3 is an example of a number line; remember that fractions and decimals are between the integers shown.

Figure 3.3. Number Line

The **opposite** of a number is the negative version of that number (or positive version if the number is negative). Remember that the distance between a number and 0 on the number line is the same as the distance between the opposite of that number and 0.

Negative numbers with larger opposites are actually smaller than negative numbers with smaller opposites. For example:

$-40 < -2.4 < 0 < 0.1 < 20$

SAMPLE QUESTION

3) To which of the following number sets does 3 NOT belong?

A. irrational

B. rational

C. whole

D. integer

Operations with Whole Numbers

Rational numbers can be used to perform mathematical operations. **Addition** is combining numbers, while **subtraction** is the process of finding the difference between numbers. Addition and subtraction are considered **inverse operations** because each operation cancels out the other operation. For example, $2 + 3 = 5$ is true, and so is the inverse, $5 - 3 = 2$.

Decomposing and composing numbers—breaking them into groupings and putting groupings back together—can help students understand the concepts of addition and subtraction. These activities can be done with numbers and manipulatives, as shown below.

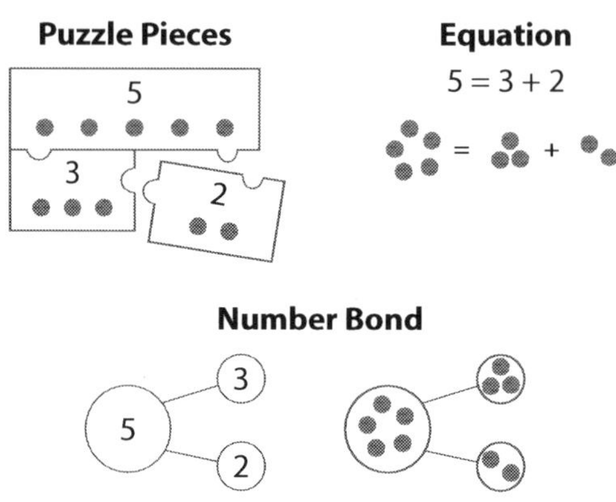

Figure 3.4. Decomposing Numbers

Multiplication is the repeated addition of the same number to itself; in contrast, **division** is splitting a number into equal parts. Multiplication and division are also inverse operations because $2 \times 3 = 6$ and the inverse, $6 \div 3 = 2$, are both true. Knowing inverse operations allows students to check their answers.

In multiplication, the two numbers multiplied together are called **factors**. The answer is called the **product**. For example, in the operation $3 \times 2 = 6$ (3 added to itself 2 times), the numbers 3 and 2 are factors, and the number 6 is the product.

Multiplication may be presented in several ways. One way to visually present a multiplication problem is with an **array**, such as the one shown below. In an array, each of the two factors is represented by the appropriate number of rows or columns, and the product will be the total number of boxes in the array.

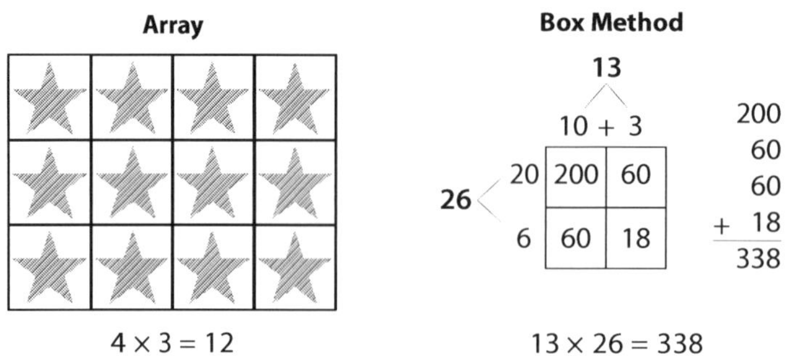

Figure 3.5. Teaching Multiplication

Another way to represent multiplication is by using **area models** (also called the box method). Although this is a non-traditional approach to multiplication, it promotes the understanding of place value.

In division, the number that is being divided into groups is called the **dividend**. The number by which the number is divided is the **divisor**. The answer is called the **quotient**. For example, in the operation $12 \div 3 = 4$, 12 is the dividend, 3 is the divisor, and 4 is the quotient.

Sometimes in a division problem, the dividend cannot be divided equally. The number that is left over when a number does not divide evenly into another number is called the **remainder**. For example, when 12 items are divided into 5 groups, each group will have 2 items in it, and there will be 2 items left over, meaning the remainder is 2.

COMMON STUDENT ERRORS

- always subtracting the smaller number from the larger number (953 – 27 = 934)
- knowing *how* to perform an operation, but not *when*
- misapplying regrouping procedures when adding or multiplying

In the figure below, 12 squares are divided into 5 different groups, each represented by a different shade of gray. There are 2 squares in each group (the quotient). Two squares are left, meaning there are not enough squares to put 3 squares in each group. Thus, the remainder is 2.

1	2	3	4
5	1	2	3
4	5		

Figure 3.6. Remainder

SAMPLE QUESTIONS

4) **A teacher has 50 notebooks to hand out to students. If she has 16 students in her class, and each student receives 2 notebooks, how many notebooks will she have left over?**

   A. 2

   B. 16

   C. 18

   D. 32

5) **A student in Miss Ward's class answers the questions as shown below.**

   1. 25 – 18 = 13

   2. 87 – 58 = 31

   3. 42 – 38 = ?

   If the student's error pattern continues, what will be their answer to question three?

A. 4
B. 14
C. 16
D. 80

Factors and Multiples

Every whole number (except 1) is either a prime number or a composite number. A **prime number** is a natural number greater than 1 that can be divided evenly only by 1 and itself. For example, 7 is a prime number because it can only be divided by the numbers 1 and 7.

On the other hand, a **composite number** is a natural number greater than 1 that can be evenly divided by at least one other number besides 1 and itself. For example, 6 is a composite number because it can be divided by 1, 2, 3, and 6. Composite numbers can be broken down into prime numbers using factor trees. For example, the number 54 is 2×27, and 27 is 3×9, and 9 is 3×3, as shown in Figure 2.6. The factor tree shows that 54 can be broken down as $54 = 2 \times 3 \times 3 \times 3$.

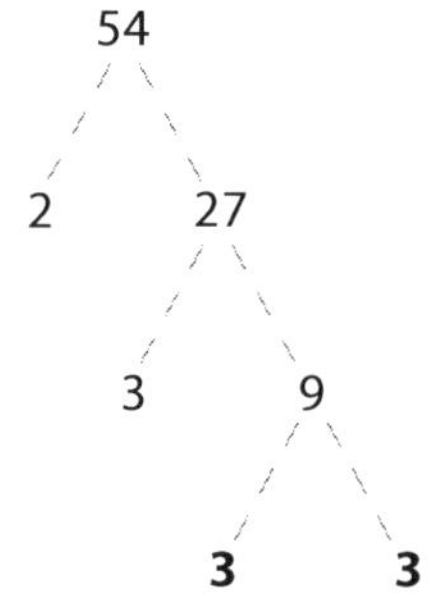

Figure 3.7. Factor Tree

The **greatest common factor (GCF)** of a set of numbers is the greatest number (other than 1) that each number in the set is divisible by without any remainders. The GCF may be one of the numbers; for example, for the numbers 4 and 8, the GCF is 4, since 4 goes into both 4 and 8. The greatest common factor can also be called the **greatest common divisor**.

To get the GCF of a set numbers, list all the prime factors of the numbers, and multiply the factors that appear on both sides. (If the factor appears twice on both sides, include both factors.) For example, the GCF of 12 and 30 is 6 because 2 and 3 are factors of both numbers:

$12 = \mathbf{2} \times 2 \times \mathbf{3}$
$30 = \mathbf{2} \times \mathbf{3} \times 5$
GCF of 12 and 30 = $2 \times 3 = 6$

The **least common multiple (LCM)** of a set of numbers is the smallest number that is a multiple of all the numbers in the set. The LCM is often called as the **least common denominator (LCD)**, especially when it is used to add and subtract fractions.

To find the LCM of numbers, find the smallest common multiple of those numbers, which is the smallest number that can be divided by both numbers without a remainder. For example, the LCM of 6 and 8 is 24, since 24 is the smallest number that is divisible by both 6 and 8. Write out all the multiples and look for the smallest number that is in both lists:

6: 6, 12, 18, **24**, 30

8: 8, 16, **24**, 32

Once the number has been broken down into its simplest form, the composite number can be expressed using exponents. An **exponent** shows how many times a number (the base) should be multiplied by itself. In the factor tree, Figure 3.7, the number 54 can be written as $2 \times 3 \times 3 \times 3$ or 2×3^3.

A **radical** is the opposite of an exponent and is an expression that has a square root, cube root, or a higher root. For example, $\sqrt{16} = 4$ since $4^2 = 16$ and $\sqrt[3]{8} = 2$ since $2^3 = 8$.

SAMPLE QUESTION

6) **What is the least common multiple of the numbers 10 and 12?**

A. 2

B. 24

C. 60

D. 120

OPERATIONS WITH POSITIVE AND NEGATIVE NUMBERS

When adding or subtracting negative numbers, look at a number line. When adding two numbers, whether they are positive or negative, count to the right; when subtracting, count to the left. Note that adding a negative value is the same as subtracting. Subtracting a negative value is the same as adding.

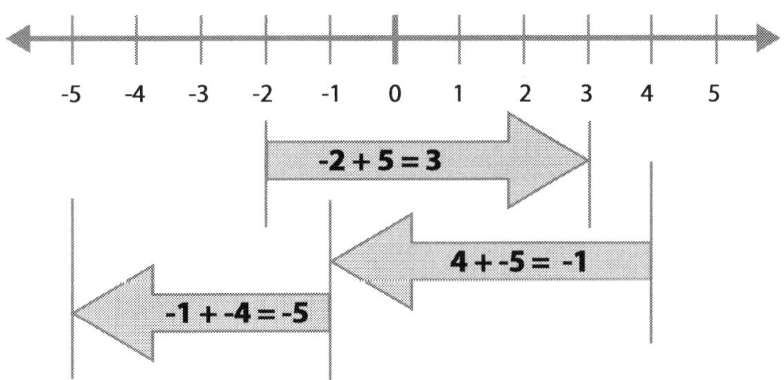

Figure 3.8. Adding Positive and Negative Numbers

Multiplying and dividing with negative and positive numbers is somewhat easier. Multiplying two numbers with the same sign gives a positive result, and multiplying two numbers with different signs gives a negative result. The same rules apply to division.

SAMPLE QUESTION

7) **Which of the following has the greatest value?**

A. $-4(3)(-2)$

B. $-16 - 17 + 31$

C. $18 - 15 + 27$

D. $-20 + 10 + 10$

Properties of Numbers and the Order of Operations

As operations become more complex there are rules, or properties, that guide the problem-solver.

Table 3.1. Mathematical Properties

Name	Description	Applies to	Example
Commutative Property	The order of the operation doesn't matter.	addition multiplication	$a + b = b + a$ $ab = ba$
Associative Property	Grouping of numbers doesn't matter.	addition multiplication	$(a + b) + c = a + (b + c)$ $(a \times b) \times c = a \times (b \times c)$
Distributive Property	Multiply a value by all the values inside brackets, then add.	multiplication	$a(b + c) = ab + ac$
Identity Property	Adding zero or multiplying by one will not change the original value.	addition multiplication	$a + 0 = a$ $a \times 1 = a$
Zero Property	Multiplying any value by zero yields a result of zero.	multiplication	$a \times 0 = 0$

When solving a multi-step equation, the **order of operations** must be used to get the correct answer. The problem should be worked in the following order: (1) parentheses and brackets, (2) exponents and square roots, (3) multiplication and division, and (4) addition and subtraction. The acronym PEMDAS can be used to remember the order of operations.

Please Excuse My Dear Aunt Sally

P – Parentheses

E – Exponents

M – Multiplication

D – Division

A – Addition

S – Subtraction

COMMON STUDENT ERRORS

- failing to apply associative property (knows $8 + 3 = 11$, but struggles to find $3 + 8$)
- thinking that subtraction and division are commutative ($9 - 4 = 4 - 9$)

The steps "Multiplication–Division" and "Addition–Subtraction" go in order from left to right. In other words, divide before multiplying if the division problem is on the left. For example, the expression $(3^2 - 2)^2 + (4)5^3$ is simplified using the following steps:

1. Parentheses: Because the parentheses in this problem contain two operations (exponents and subtraction) use the order of operations within the parentheses. Exponents come before subtraction.
   $(3^2 - 2)^2 + (4)5^3 = (9 - 2)^2 + (4)5^3 = (7)^2 + (4)5^3$
2. Exponents: $(7)^2 + (4)5^3 = 49 + (4)125$
3. Multiplication and division: $49 + (4)125 = 49 + 500$
4. Addition and subtraction: $49 + 500 = 549$

SAMPLE QUESTIONS

8) **Which expression is equivalent to dividing 400 by 16?**
   A. 2(200 – 8)
   B. (400 ÷ 4) ÷ 12
   C. (216 ÷ 8) + (184 ÷ 8)
   D. (216 ÷ 16) + (184 ÷ 16)

9) **Which prerequisite skill should students master before learning the associative property?**
   A. order of operations
   B. simplifying two-step equations
   C. multiplication
   D. adding fractions

PLACE VALUE AND DECIMALS

PLACE VALUE

While historically some civilizations have used other numbering systems, today most of the world uses the base-10 system. In the **base-10** system, each **digit** (the numeric symbols 0 – 9) in a number is worth ten times as much as the number to the right of it.

Table 3.2. Place Value Chart

100,000	10,000	1,000	100	10	1		1/10	1/100
10^5	10^4	10^3	10^2	10^1	10^0	.	10^{-1}	10^{-2}
hundred thousands	ten thousands	thousands	hundreds	tens	ones	decimal	tenths	hundredths

For example, in the number 37 each digit has a different value based on its location. This is called **place value.** The 3 is in the tens place, and so has a value of 30, and the 7 is in the ones place, so it has a value of 7.

A **decimal** is any real number in the base-10 system, but it often refers to numbers with digits to the right of the decimal point.

COMMON STUDENT ERRORS

- misunderstanding how to expand numbers (306 = 30 + 6)
- ordering numbers based on the value of the digits instead of place value (57 > 103)
- transcribing spoken numbers incorrectly (three thousand four hundred and twelve = 3000,400,12)

Knowing the place value of each digit allows students to write a number in expanded form. **Expanded form** is breaking up a number by the value of each digit. For example, the expanded form of 321 is written as 300 + 20 + 1. This proces is also called **decomposing** a number. The alternate process—building a number from expanded form—is **composing** a number.

50	4	.	0.3	0.02
Tens	Ones	Decimal Point	Tenths	Hundredths
50 + 4 + 0.3 + 0.02 = 54.32				

Figure 3.9. Decomposing Decimals

SAMPLE QUESTIONS

10) **Which digit is in the hundredths place when 1.3208 is divided by 5.2?**

A. 0

B. 4

C. 5

D. 8

11) **Which number has the greatest value?**

A. 9,299 ones

B. 903 tens

C. 93 hundreds

D. 9 thousands

Rounding Numbers

Rounding is used to make numbers easier to work with. The process makes numbers less accurate, but makes operations and mental math easier.

To round a number, first identify the digit in the specified place (such as the tens or hundreds). Then look at the digit one place to the right. If that digit is four or less, keep the digit in the specified place the same. If that digit is five or more, add 1 to the digit in the specified place. All the digits to the right of the specified place become zeros.

Numbers can be rounded to any place value:

- rounded to the hundreds place: 5,372 → 5,400
- rounded to the tens place: 5,372 → 5,370
- rounded to the tenths place: 11.635 → 11.600
- rounded to the hundredths place: 11.635 → 11.640

COMMON STUDENT ERRORS

decreasing the number in the specified place when rounding down (1<u>6</u>3 → 1<u>5</u>0)

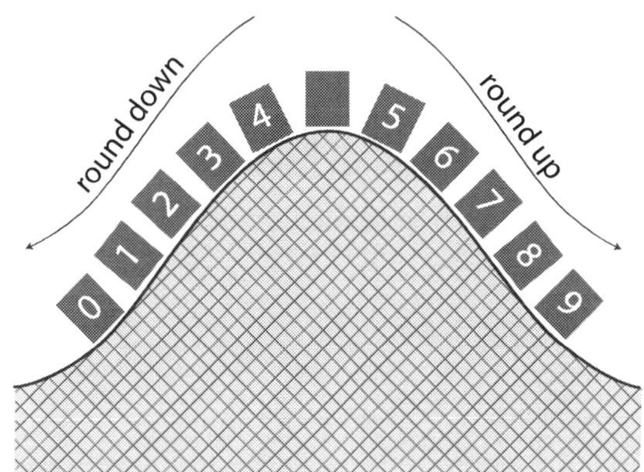

Figure 3.10. Rounding

SAMPLE QUESTION

12) What is 498,235 rounded to the nearest thousands?

A. 498,000

B. 498,200

C. 499,000

D. 500,000

FRACTIONS AND RATIOS

FRACTIONS

Fractions use two numbers separated by a horizontal bar to show parts of a whole. Fractions include a **numerator**, the number on top of a fraction, and a **denominator**, the number on the bottom of a fraction. The denominator is the "whole," and the numerator is the "part." For example, if there are 12 students on the chess team, and 5 of the students are

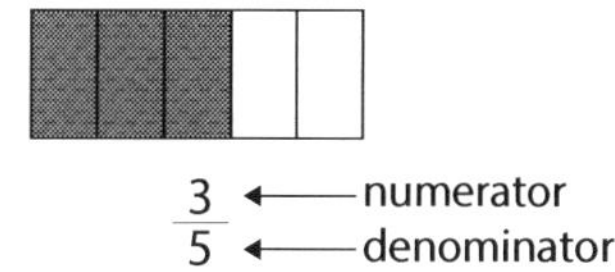

$\frac{3}{5}$ ← numerator ← denominator

Figure 3.11. Parts of a Fraction

selected to represent the school in a tournament, the fraction of the chess team going to the tournament is $\frac{5}{12}$.

If the numerator of a fraction is 1, it is called a **unit fraction**. In the chess team example, $\frac{1}{12}$ is the unit fraction. Five $\frac{1}{12}$ units represent the part of the team that is going to the tournament. As the "whole" gets larger, one "part" becomes smaller and smaller. Think of cutting a cake: cutting 8 slices creates smaller slices than cutting the same cake into 4 slices. So, as the denominator of unit fractions increases, the value of the fraction itself decreases.

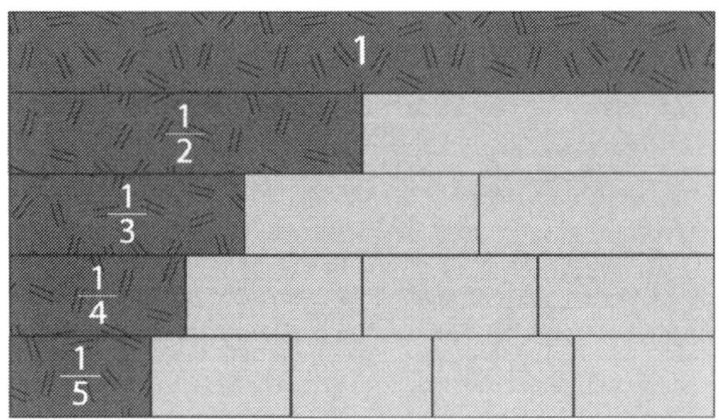

Figure 3.12. Unit Fractions

Fractions have several forms:

- **proper fraction**: the numerator is less than the denominator
- **improper fraction**: the numerator is greater than or equal to the denominator
- **mixed number**: the combination of a whole number and a fraction

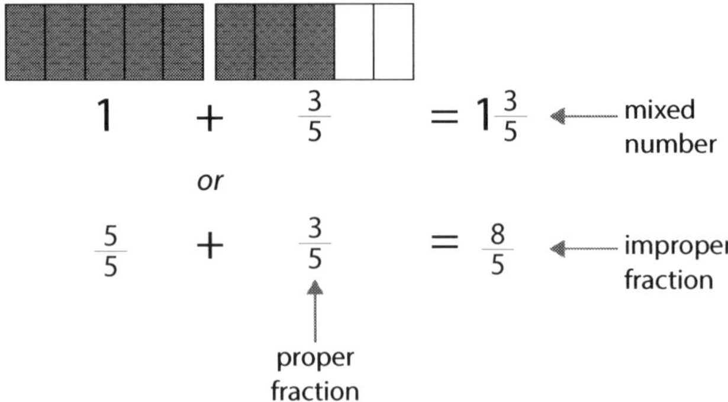

Figure 3.13. Types of Fractions

Improper fractions can be converted to mixed numbers by dividing. The quotient becomes the whole number, and the remainder becomes the new numerator:

$$\frac{17}{5} = 3\frac{2}{5}$$

To convert a mixed number to a fraction, multiply the whole number by the denominator of the fraction, and add the numerator. The result becomes the numerator of the improper fraction; the denominator remains the same:

$$5\frac{3}{4} = \frac{(5 \times 4 + 3)}{4} = \frac{23}{4}$$

A fraction is in **lowest terms** (or **reduced**) when the numerator and the denominator have no common factors other than 1. Reduce fractions to lowest terms by dividing both the numerator and denominator by their greatest common factor:

$$\frac{16}{24} = \frac{(16 \div 8)}{(24 \div 8)} = \frac{2}{3}$$

Fractions are **equivalent**, or equal, when they reduce to the same fraction. For example, the fractions $\frac{2}{8}$, $\frac{4}{16}$, and $\frac{8}{32}$ are equivalent because they all reduce to $\frac{1}{4}$.

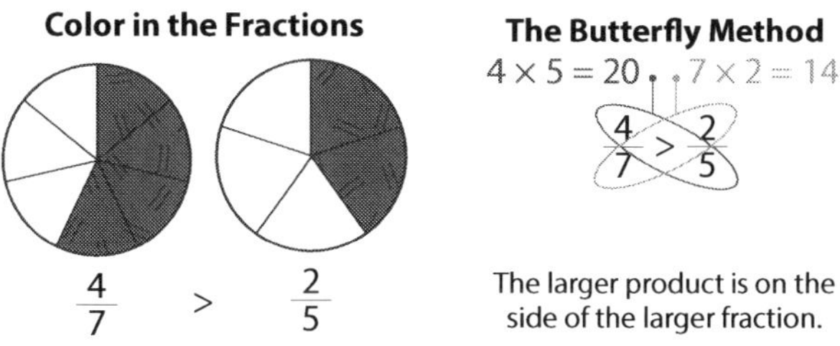

Figure 3.14. Comparing Fractions

When fractions are not equivalent, once must necessarily be larger than the other. There are a number of methods students can use to compare fractions:

- coloring visual representation of fractions
- cross multiplying (the butterly method)
- placing the fractions on a number line
- finding a common denominator

SAMPLE QUESTIONS

13) Amanda is having difficulty adding fractions with unlike denominators. With which of the following does Amanda need support?

A. how to simplify an exponent

B. how to multiply decimals

C. how to find the least common multiple

D. how to solve a multi-step equation

14) Carla divides her pizza into 8 equal slices and takes 1 piece. If the amount of pizza remaining is written as a fraction, the numerator will be.

A. 1

B. 7

C. 8

D. 9

Operations with Fractions

The same basic operations that can be performed with whole numbers can also be performed on fractions, with a few modifications. When adding and subtracting fractions, each fraction must have a **common denominator**. The operation is performed in the numerator, and the denominator remains the same. For example, if $\frac{3}{12}$ of the chess team described above is eliminated in the second round of the tournament, the total fraction of the team remaining will be:

$$\frac{5}{12} - \frac{3}{12} = \frac{5-3}{12} = \frac{2}{12}$$

In $\frac{2}{12}$, both the numerator and the denominator are divisible by 2, meaning the fraction is not in its simplest form. To simplify the fraction, reduce the numerator and denominator by dividing both by the same value:

$$\frac{2}{12} = \frac{2 \div 2}{12 \div 2} = \frac{1}{6}$$

If the fractions to be added or subtracted do not have a common denominator, the **least common multiple** of the denominators (also known as the **least common denominator**) must be found. In the operation $\frac{2}{3} - \frac{1}{2}$, the common denominator will be a **multiple** of both 3 and 2. Multiples are found by multiplying the denominator by whole numbers until a common multiple is found:

- multiples of 3 are **3** (3 × 1), **6** (3 × 2), **9** (3 × 3), ...
- multiples of 2 are **2** (2 × 1), **4** (2 × 2), **6** (2 × 3), ...

Since 6 is the smallest multiple of both 3 and 2, it is the least common multiple and can be used as the common denominator. Both the numerator and denominator of each fraction should be multiplied by the appropriate whole number:

$$\frac{2}{3}\left(\frac{2}{2}\right) - \frac{1}{2}\left(\frac{3}{3}\right) = \frac{4}{6} - \frac{3}{6} = \frac{1}{6}$$

When multiplying fractions, simply multiply each numerator together and each denominator together. To divide two fractions, invert the second fraction (swap the numerator and denominator) then multiply normally.

- $\frac{5}{6} \times \frac{2}{3} = \frac{10}{18} = \frac{5}{9}$
- $\frac{5}{6} \div \frac{2}{3} = \frac{5}{6} \times \frac{3}{2} = \frac{15}{12} = \frac{5}{4}$

Fractions can be converted to decimals by simply dividing the denominator by the numerator. To convert a decimal to a fraction, place the numbers to the right of

COMMON STUDENT ERRORS

- making the shaded region the numerator and the unshaded region the denominator
- thinking that the fraction with the larger denominator is larger $\left(\frac{1}{5} > \frac{1}{3}\right)$
- always dividing by 2 to reduce fractions $\left(\frac{7}{10} = \frac{3.5}{5}\right)$
- adding the numerator and the denominators $\left(\frac{1}{3} + \frac{2}{5} = \frac{3}{8}\right)$
- misunderstanding the relationship between the fraction bar and the decimal $\left(\frac{3}{5} = 3.5 \text{ or } 0.35\right)$

the decimal over the appropriate base-10 power and simplify the fraction. To convert a decimal to a percentage, multiply the decimal by 100, or move the decimal point two digits to the right. To convert a percentage to a decimal, divide by 100, or move the decimal point two digits to the left.

- $\frac{1}{2} = 1 \div 2 = 0.5$
- $0.375 = \frac{375}{1,000} = \frac{3}{8}$

SAMPLE QUESTIONS

15) **Simplify:** $\left(1\frac{1}{2}\right)\left(2\frac{2}{3}\right) \div 1\frac{1}{4}$

A. $3\frac{1}{12}$

B. $3\frac{1}{5}$

C. 4

D. 5

16) **Students need to understand how to find a least common multiple when**

A. adding fractions with unlike denominators.

B. adding fractions with unlike numerators.

C. multiplying fractions with unlike denominators.

D. dividing fractions with unlike numerators.

PROPORTIONAL RELATIONSHIPS

Ratios compare two things. For example, if Jamie has 6 pairs of jeans and 8 T-shirts, then the ratio of jeans to T-shirts is 6:8. Like fractions, ratios can be reduced when both values are multiples of the same number. For example, the ratio 6:8 can be reduced by dividing both parts by 2: 6:8 = 3:4. The value of the ratio doesn't change because a ratio only describes a relationship. Whether Jamie has 3 jeans and 4 shirts; 6 jeans and 8 shirts; or 12 jeans and 16 shirts, the ratio remains the same. In other words, for every 3 pairs of jeans Jamie has, she has 4 T-shirts.

Problems involving ratios can often be solved by setting up a **proportion**, which is an equation stating that two ratios are equal. For example, if Jamie wants to buy 9 pairs of jeans and maintain the ratio described above, a proportion can be used to find the number of shirts she'll need to purchase: $\frac{jeans}{T\text{-}shirts} = \frac{3}{4} = \frac{9}{x}$.

The two fractions can then be **cross-multiplied** to give the equation $3x = 36$, and the variable isolated: $x = 12$ shirts.

When working with ratios, pay attention to whether part-to-part or part-to-whole comparisons are being used. For example, if there are 6 boys and 4 girls in a class, the ratio of boys to girls is 6:4, but the ratio of boys to the total is 6:10.

HELPFUL HINT

cross-multiplication:
$\frac{a}{b} = \frac{c}{d} \rightarrow ad = bc$

SAMPLE QUESTION

17) **If a car uses 8 gallons of gas to travel 650 miles, how many miles can it travel using 12 gallons of gas?**

A. 870 miles

B. 895 miles

C. 915 miles

D. 975 miles

Early Equations and Expressions

Algebraic Expressions

Algebraic thinking introduces students to **variables**, which are symbols that represent unknown amounts. Variables are usually represented with letters, although boxes or other symbols can be used.

Algebraic expressions contain numbers, variables, and at least one mathematical operation. Each group of numbers and variables in an expression is called a **term** (e.g., $3x$ or $16y$). An expression describes a mathematical relationship. For example, the expression $2x + 4$ means "multiply x by 2 and add 4." Note that an expreesion does not include an equal sign.

Table 3.3. Building Algebraic Expressions

Operation	Key Words	Example
Addition	added, and, plus, total, increased, combined, sum, together	a number increased by 5 $x + 5x$
Subtraction	decrease, take away, give away, fewer, minus, difference, less	8 fewer than a number $x - 8$
Multiplication	times, increased by a factor, doubled, tripled	triple a number $3x$
Division	per, ratio, divided, split into, quotient, half	a number split into 4 groups $x \div 4$
Parentheses	twice sum of, three times the difference of	three times the sum of 2 numbers $3(x + y)$

Algebraic expressions can be evaluated for a specific value by plugging that value into the expression and simplifying. When $x = 5$, the expression $2x + 4 = 2(5) + 4 = 14$.

To add or subtract algebraic expressions, add the variables and numbers (constants) separately. For example, $(5x - 3) + (3x - 2) = (5x + 3x) + (-3 - 2) = 8x - 5$. Only terms with the same variable(s), called **like terms**, can be combined.

SAMPLE QUESTIONS

18) If $x = 5$, what is the value of the algebraic expression $2x - 3$?

A. 5

B. 7

C. 12

D. 15

19) Sawyer has c pieces of Halloween candy in her bucket. She gives 4 pieces of candy to a friend and splits the remaining candy with her sister. Which expression describes how many pieces of candy Sawyer now has?

A. $2(c - 4)$

B. $(c - 4) \div 2$

C. $2(c + 4)$

D. $(c + 4) \div 2$

ALGEBRAIC EQUATIONS

In an **equation**, two expressions are joined by an equal sign, which indicates that the two expressions are equal to each other. The two sides of an equation act like a balanced scale: operations can be performed on equations as long as the same operation is performed on both sides to maintain the balance.

This property can be used to solve the equation by performing operations that isolate the variable on one side. For example, the equation $4x + 12 = 2x + 48$ can be solved for x using the following steps:

COMMON STUDENT ERRORS

- adding a constant to a variable ($5 + 3x = 8x$)
- not combing like terms ($4x + 3x - 6$)
- thinking a variable can only stand for one number

1. Subtract 12 from both sides of the equation:
$(4x + 12) - 12 = (2x + 48) - 12$
$4x = 2x + 36$
2. Subtract $2x$ from both sides of the equation:
$(4x) - 2x = (2x + 36) - 2x$
$2x = 36$
3. Divide both sides by 2:
$\frac{2x}{2} = \frac{36}{2}$
$x = 18$

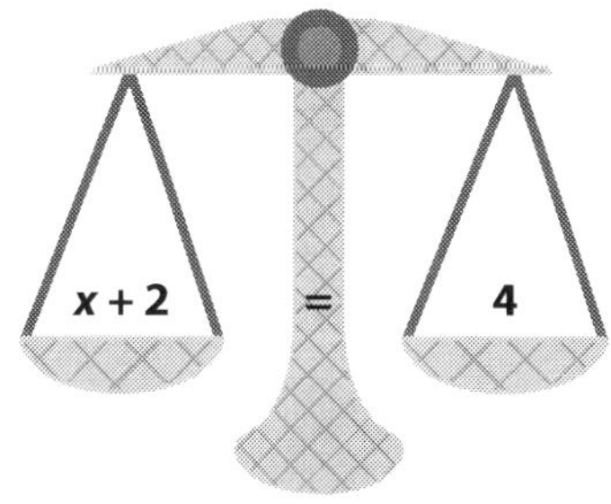

Figure 3.15. Equations

SAMPLE QUESTIONS

20) Solve for x: $5x - 4 = 3(8 + 3x)$

A. -7

B. $-\frac{3}{4}$

C. $\frac{3}{4}$

D. 7

21) When introducing equations to students, which step should Ms. Martin take first?

A. assign students to work with a partner to solve $3x + 5 = 20$ on whiteboards

B. assign students to work individually to solve $3x + 5 = 20$ on paper

C. assign students to work with a partner to draw a picture representing $3x + 5 = 20$

D. assign students to use mats and counters to demonstrate $3x + 5 = 20$

INEQUALITIES

Inequalities are similar to equations, but both sides of the problem are not equal (≠). Inequalities may be represented as follows: greater than (>), greater than or equal to (≥), less than (<), or less than or equal to (≤).

Inequalities may be represented on a number line, as shown below. A circle is placed on the end point with a filled circle representing ≤ and ≥, and an empty circle representing < and >. An arrow is then drawn to show either all the values greater than or less than 3.

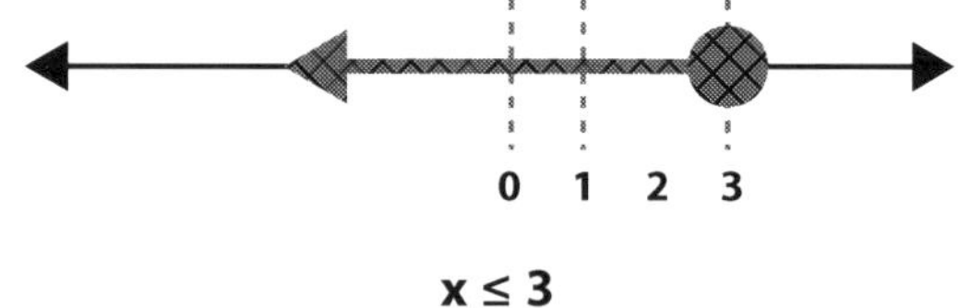

Figure 3.16. Inequality Line Graph

Inequalities can be solved by manipulating them much like equations. However, the solution to an inequality is a set of numbers, not a single value. For example, simplifying $4x + 2 \leq 14$ gives the inequality $x \leq 3$, meaning every number less than 3 or equal to 3 would be included in the set of correct answers.

SAMPLE QUESTION

22) Which of the following is a solution to the inequality $2x + y \leq -10$?

A. (0, 0)

B. (10, 2)

C. (10, 10)

D. (−10, −10)

MEASUREMENT

Measurement includes length, weight, capacity, and time. Before learning to use standard measurement tools such as rulers or scales, students should understand the basic concepts of measurement using nonstandard measurement tools like blocks, erasers, and even fingers. Basic concepts of measure, such as comparing lengths and weights, have more meaning to students when everyday objects are used.

Once students have a basic understanding of measurement, conversions can be introduced using **nonstandard tools**. For example, measure the length of a desk using a thumb. Then measure the length of a desk using an unsharpened pencil. Will the student need more thumbs or more pencils to measure the desk? How many thumbs equal a pencil?

Discuss vocabulary words such as *measure, scale, balance, length, weight, capacity, short* (*–er, –est*), *long* (*–er, –est*) *more*, and *less*; students will gain a clear understanding of these terms by engaging in various measurement activities. These activities include estimating and then determining the length of items such as pencils, crayons, scissors, books, desks, and even students themselves using standard and nonstandard units of measure and ordering objects from least to greatest and greatest to least. Students can also use scales and balances to weigh various objects and to explore relationships between different objects (which objects are heavier, lighter, heaviest, and lightest).

The standard units for the metric and American systems are shown below, along with the prefixes used to express metric units.

Table 3.4. Units and Conversion Factors

Dimension	American	SI
length	inch/foot/yard/mile	meter
mass	ounce/pound/ton	kilogram
volume	cup/pint/quart/gallon	liter
force	pound-force	newton
pressure	pound-force per square inch	pascal
work and energy	cal/British thermal unit	joule
temperature	Fahrenheit	kelvin
charge	faraday	coulomb

Table 3.5. Metric Prefixes

Prefix	Symbol	Multiplication Factor
tera	T	1,000,000,000,000
giga	G	1,000,000,000
mega	M	1,000,000
kilo	k	1,000
hecto	h	100
deca	da	10
base unit	--	--
deci	d	0.1
centi	c	0.01
milli	m	0.001
micro	µ	0.0000001
nano	n	0.0000000001
pico	p	0.0000000000001

Units can be converted within a single system or between systems. When converting from one unit to another unit, a **conversion factor** (a numeric multiplier used to convert a value with a unit to another unit) is used. The process of converting between units using a conversion factor is sometimes known as **dimensional analysis**.

Table 3.6. Conversion Factors

1 in. = 2.54 cm	1 lb. = 0.454 kg
1 yd. = 0.914 m	1 cal = 4.19 J
1 mi. = 1.61 km	$1°F = \frac{5}{9}(°F - 32°C)$
1 gal. = 3.785 L	1 cm^3 = 1 mL
1 oz. = 28.35 g	1 hr = 3600 s

SAMPLE QUESTIONS

23) Convert the following measurements:

A. 4.25 kilometers to meters

B. 8 m^2 to mm^2

C. 12 feet to inches

D. 23 meters to feet

24) **How much longer is line segment MN than line segment KL?**

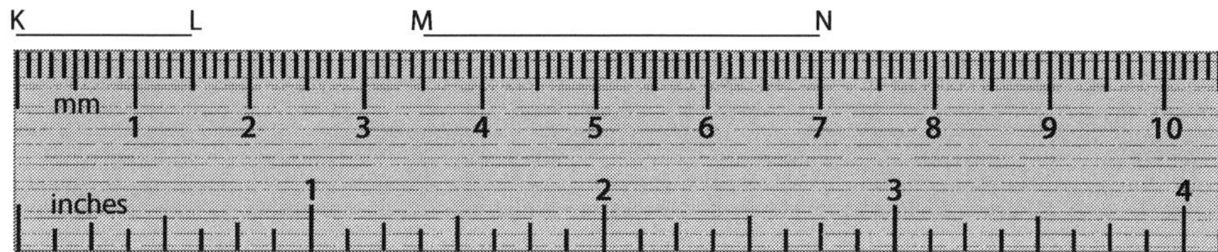

A. 15 mm

B. 20 mm

C. 2 mm

D. 55 mm

GEOMETRY

LINES AND ANGLES

Geometric figures are shapes comprised of points, lines, or planes. A **point** is simply a location in space; it does not have any dimensional properties such as length, area, or volume. A collection of points that extends infinitely in both directions is a **line**, and one that extends infinitely in only one direction is a **ray**. A section of a line with a beginning and end is a **line segment**. Lines, rays, and line segments are examples of **one-dimensional** objects because they can only be measured in one dimension (length).

> HELPFUL HINT
>
> While you're reviewing content topics for the test, think about engaging students with different learning styles. For example, when teaching angles, you can:
>
> - engage **kinesthetic** learners by having students name the angles they form doing sit-ups
> - engage **auditory** learners with songs that list the types of angles
> - engage **visual** learners by having students make angles with popsicle sticks

Lines, rays, and line segments can intersect to create **angles**, which are measured in degrees or radians. Angles between 0 and 90 degrees are **acute**, and angles between 90 and 180 degrees are **obtuse**. An angle of exactly 90 degrees is a **right angle**, and two lines that form right angles are **perpendicular**. Lines that do not intersect are described as **parallel**.

Two angles with measurements that add up to 90 degrees are **complementary**, and two angles with measurements that add up to 180 degrees are **supplementary**. Two adjacent (touching) angles are called a **linear pair**, and they are supplementary.

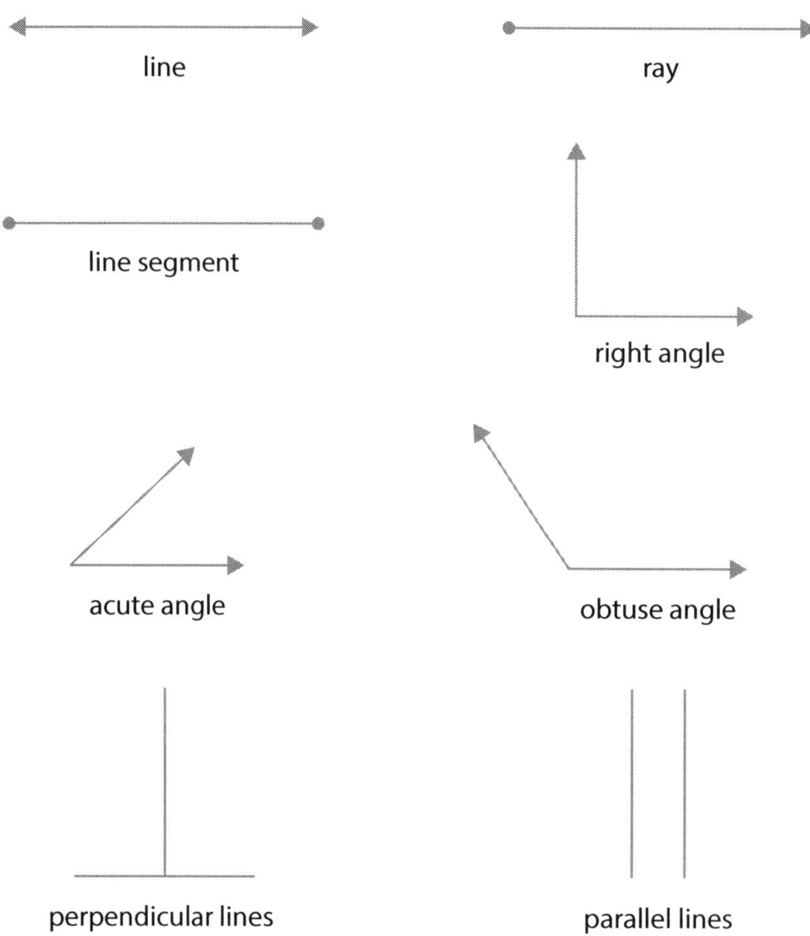

Figure 3.17. Lines and Angles

SAMPLE QUESTION

25) Mrs. Cortez is working with her students on comparing angles. A worksheet includes a picture of the following angle and asks students to draw a larger angle.

Which of the following student answers is correct?

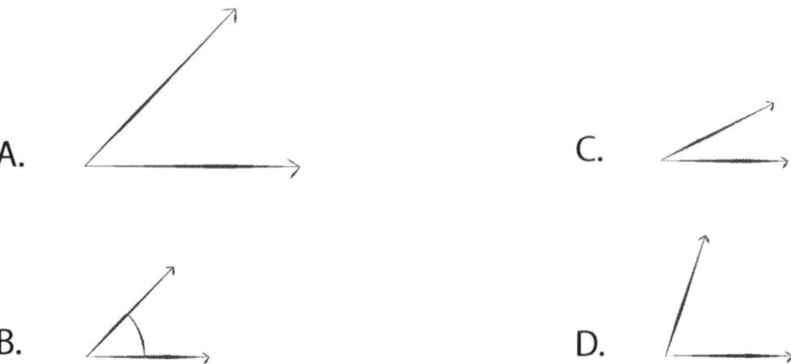

PLANE SHAPES

Two-dimensional objects can be measured in two dimensions (length and width). A **plane** is a two-dimensional object that extends infinitely in both dimensions. **Polygons** are two-dimensional shapes, such as triangles and squares, that have three or more straight sides. **Regular polygons** are polygons with sides that are all the same length.

Students must have a clear understanding of these **plane shapes** before they can move on to working with three-dimensional shapes. Students should use attribute blocks and pattern blocks to begin their study of plane shapes. Sorting the shapes according to different attributes helps students gain a clear understanding of important terms, including *sides, edges, corners, vertices,* and *faces.*

Students should construct a **plane shape anchor chart** identifying each shape, its number of sides, corners, and faces, and some real-world examples. Learning activities include identifying, naming, and describing the shapes; sorting shapes according to different attributes; comparing them by determining differences and similarities; examining symmetry; and creating pictures out of shapes.

Shape	Sides Angles	Looks Like
Circle 	no flat side no angles	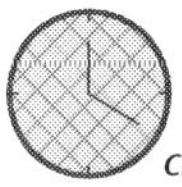 *clock*
Triangle 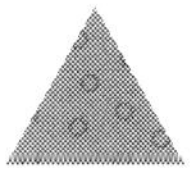	3 sides 3 angles	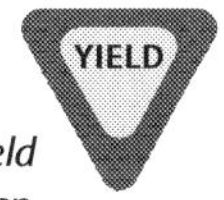 YIELD *yield sign*
Square	4 sides 4 angles	 Q W E R A S *keyboard keys*
Rectangle 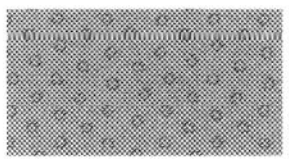	4 sides 4 angles	*TV* 
Hexagon 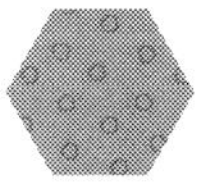	6 sides 6 angles	 *white shapes in soccer ball*

Figure 3.18. Plane Shape Anchor Chart

A **circle** is the set of all the points in a plane that are the same distance from a fixed point (called the center). The distance from the center to any point on the circle is the **radius** of the circle. The **diameter** is the largest measurement across a circle. It passes through the circle's center, extending from one side of the circle to the other. The measure of the diameter is twice the measure of the radius.

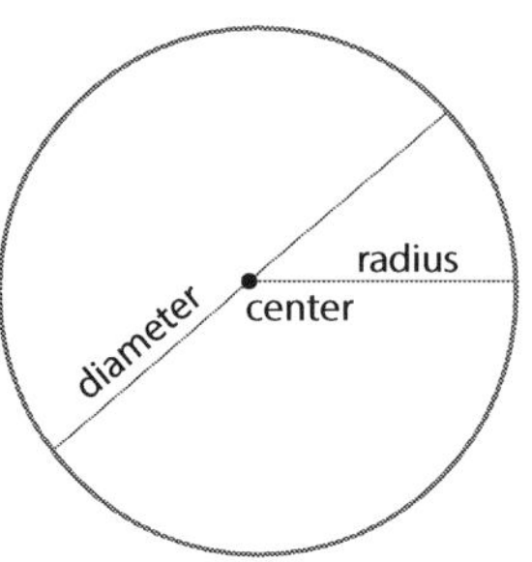

Figure 3.19. Parts of a Circle

Triangles have three sides and three interior angles that always sum to 180°. A **scalene triangle** has no equal sides or angles. An **isosceles triangle** has two equal sides and two equal angles (often called base angles). In an **equilateral triangle**, all three sides are equal as are all three angles. Moreover, because the sum of the angles of a triangle is always 180°, each angle of an equilateral triangle must be 60°.

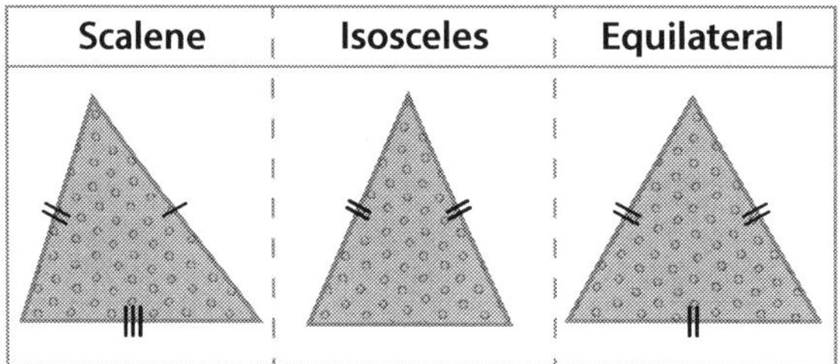

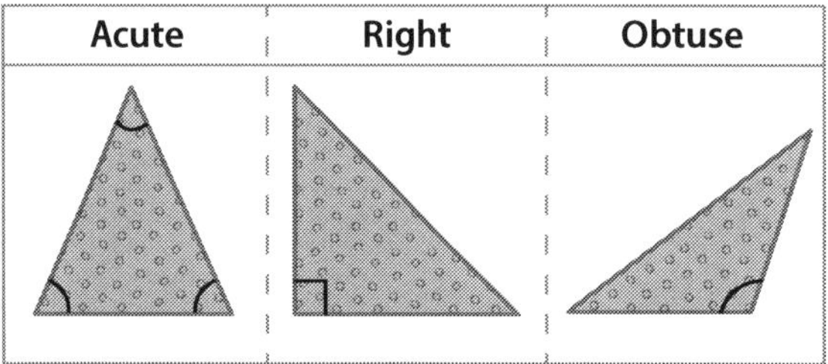

Figure 3.20. Types of Triangles

Quadrilaterals have four sides and four angles. In a **rectangle**, each of the four angles measures 90° and there are two pairs of sides with equal lenghts. A **square** also have four 90° angles, and all four of its sides are an equal length.

The **length**, or distance from one point to another on an object, can be determined using a tape measure or a ruler. The size of the surface of a two-dimensional object is its **area**. The distance around a two-dimensional figure is its **perimeter**, which can be found by adding the lengths of all the sides.

COMMON STUDENT ERRORS

- confusing area and perimeter
- using the formulas for rectangles on nonrectagular quadrilaterals

Table 3.7. Area and Perimeter of Basic Shapes

Shape	Areas	Perimeter	Variables
Triangle	$A = \frac{1}{2}bh$	$P = s_1 + s_2 + s_3$	b = base h = height s = side l = length w = width r = radius C = circumference
Square	$A = s^2$	$P = 4s$	
Rectangle	$A = l \times w$	$P = 2l + 2w$	
Circle	$A = \pi r^2$	$C = 2\pi r$	

For the rectangle below, the area would be 8 m^2 because 2 m × 4 m = 8 m^2. The perimeter of the rectangle would be 12 meters because the sum of the length of all sides is 2 m + 4 m + 2 m + 4 m = 12 m.

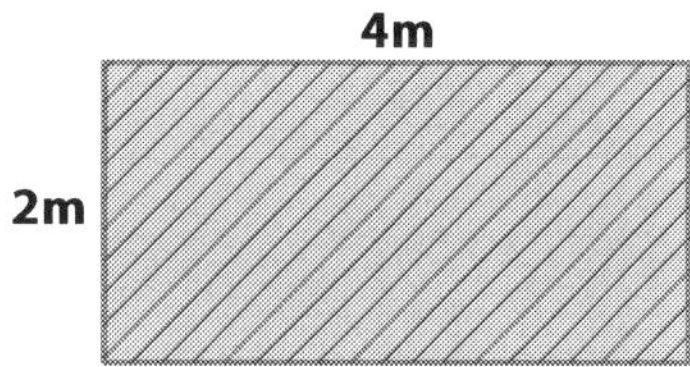

Figure 3.21. Rectangle

SAMPLE QUESTIONS

26) What is the area of the shape shown below?

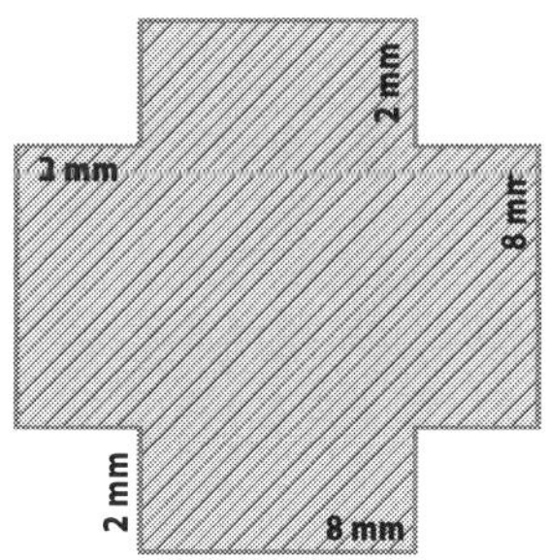

A. 64 mm^2

B. 16 mm^2

C. 128 mm^2

D. 6 mm^2

27) Miss Meriwether asks her students to find the perimeter of the triangle below. Which student correctly finds the perimeter?

A. Jan multiplies 2 × 3 × 4.

B. Jack multiplies 2 × 3, then divides by 2.

C. Molly adds 2 + 3 + 4.

D. Matthew multiplies 4 × 3, then divides by 2.

Solid Shapes

Three-dimensional objects, such as cubes, can be measured in three dimensions (length, width, and height). Three-dimensional objects are also called **solids**, and the shape of a flattened solid is called a **net**.

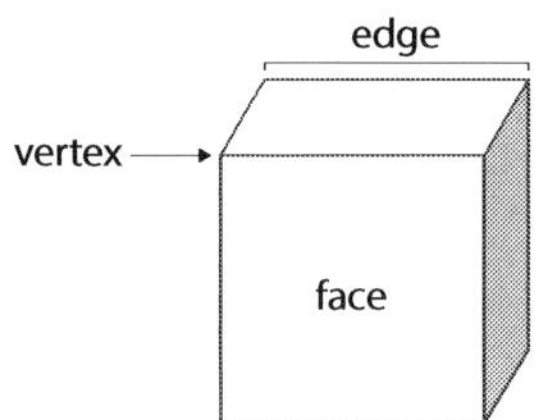

Figure 3.22. Parts of a Solid

As with plane shapes, students should construct a **solid shape anchor chart** (Figure 3.24) identifying each shape and its number of sides, corners, and faces; real world examples of each shape should be included as well. Students should engage in the same types of activities as used for learning about plane shapes. Other fun activities for students include stamping or tracing solid shapes to determine the face of each shape, sorting real-world examples of each shape into solid shape categories, and using the attributes and properties of the shapes to create new shapes.

The **surface area** of a three-dimensional object can be figured by adding the areas of all the sides. For example, the box below is 4 feet long, 3 feet wide, and 1 foot deep. The surface area is found by adding the areas of each face:

Shape	Net	Faces Vertices	Looks Like
Sphere	can't be flattened	1 curved face no vertices	*baseball* *balloon* *the moon*
Cube		6 faces 8 vertices	*dice* *ice cube*
Rectangular Prism		6 faces 8 vertices	*lego* *book* *box*
Pyramid		5 faces 5 vertices	*pyramids in Egypt*
Cylinder		2 flat faces 1 curved face	*cup* *soda can* *marker*
Cone		1 flat face 1 curved face	*ice cream cone* *party hat*

Figure 3.23. Solid Shape Anchor Chart

- top: 4 ft. × 3 ft. = 12 ft^2
- bottom: 4 ft. × 3 ft. = 12 ft^2
- front: 4 ft. × 1 ft. = 4 ft^2
- back: 4 ft. × 1 ft. = 4 ft^2
- right: 3 ft. × 1 ft. = 3 ft^2
- left: 3 ft. × 1 ft. = 3 ft^2

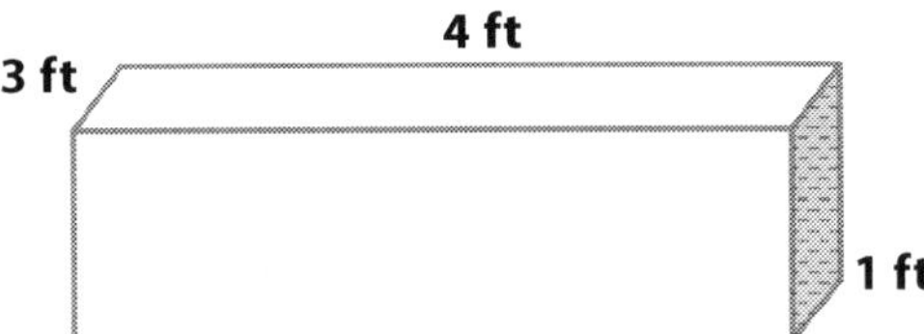

Figure 3.24. Surface Area

A **net** (flattened out three-dimensional solid) can also be used to find the surface area of solids. For example, for a square pyramid with a base with side 6 m and slant height (height in the middle of the triangular faces) of 8 m, the surface area can be calculated with a square and four triangles:

Surface Area = Area of Square Base + Area of 4 Triangles = $6^2 + 4\left[\frac{1}{2}(6 \times 8)\right]$ = 36 + 96 = 132 m^2.

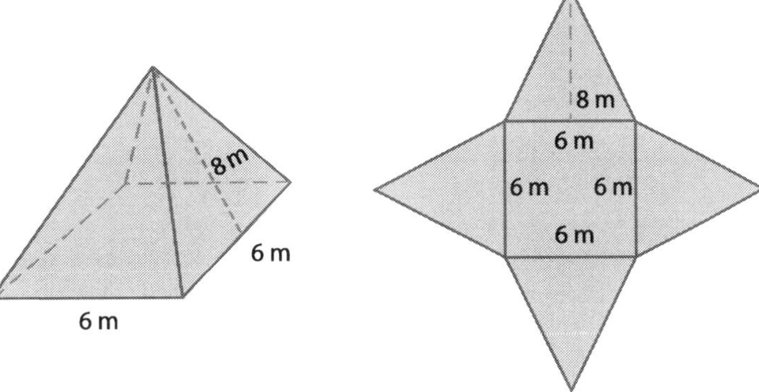

Figure 3.25. Surface Area of a Pyramid

Volume is the amount of space that a three-dimensional object takes up. Volume is measured in cubic units (e.g., ft^3 or mm^3). The volume of a solid can be determined by multiplying length times width times height. In the rectangular prism below, the volume is 3 in. × 1 in. × 1 in. = 3 in^3.

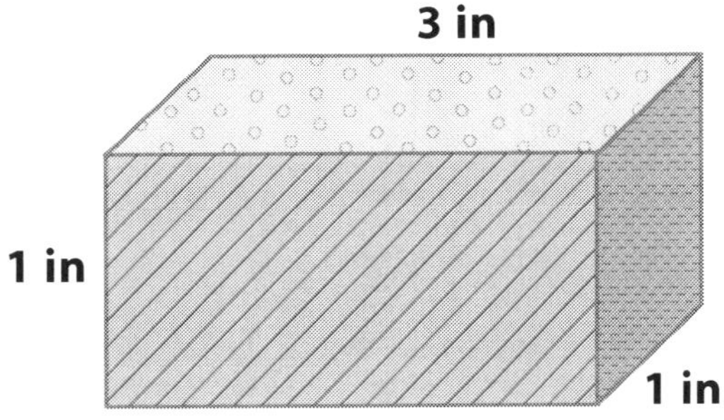

Figure 3.26. Volume

Solid	Volume	Surface Area	Variables
Sphere	$V = \frac{4}{3}\pi r^3$	$SA = 4\pi r^2$	r = radius s = side h = height l = length B = base area w = width
Cube	$V = s^3$	$SA = 6s^2$	
Cylinder	$V = \pi r^2 h$	$SA = 2\pi rh + 2\pi r^2$	
Right Rectangular Prism	$V = Bh$	$SA = 2lw + 2hw + 2hl$	

Table 3.8. Area and Volume of Basic Solids

SAMPLE QUESTION

28) Which three-dimensional solid has 4 triangular faces and 1 square face?

A. pyramid

B. cube

C. rectangular prism

D. cylinder

Graphing on a Coordinate Plane

A **coordinate plane** is a plane containing the x- and y-axes. The **x-axis** is the horizontal line on a graph where $y = 0$. The **y-axis** is the vertical line on a graph where $x = 0$. The x-axis and y-axis intersect to create four **quadrants**. The first quadrant is in the upper right, and other quadrants are labeled counter-clockwise using the roman numerals I, II, III, and IV. **Points**, or locations, on the graph are written as **ordered pairs**, (x,y), with the point (0,0) called the **origin**. Points are plotted by counting over x places from the origin horizontally and y places from the origin vertically.

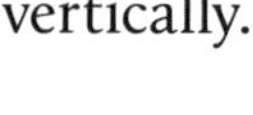

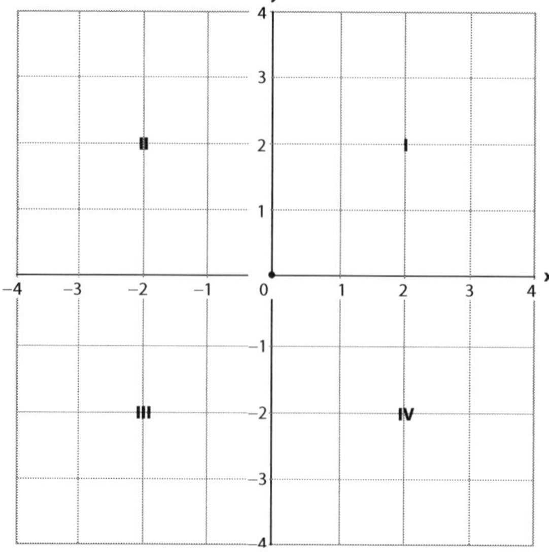

Figure 3.28. Four Quadrants

SAMPLE QUESTION

29) In which quadrant is the point (–5, 2) located?

A. I

B. II

C. III

D. IV

DATA ANALYSIS

STATISTICS

Statistics is the study of data. Analyzing data requires using **measures of center** (mean, median, and mode) to identify trends or patterns.

The **mean** is the average; it is determined by adding all outcomes and then dividing by the total number of outcomes. For example, the average of the data set {16, 19, 19, 25, 27, 29, 75} is equal to $\frac{16 + 19 + 19 + 25 + 27 + 29 + 75}{7} = \frac{210}{7} = 30$.

The **median** is the number in the middle when the data set is arranged in order from least to greatest. For example, in the data set {16, 19, 19, **25**, 27, 29, 75}, the median is 25. When a data set contains an even number of values, finding the median requires averaging the two middle values. In the data set {75, 80, 82, 100}, the two numbers in the middle are 80 and 82. Consequently, the median will be the average of these two values: $\frac{80 + 82}{2} = 81$.

HELPFUL HINT

Mode is most common. Median is in the middle (like a median in the road). Mean is average.

Finally, the **mode** is the most frequent outcome in a data set. In the set {16, 19, 19, 25, 27, 29, 75}, the mode is 19 because it occurs twice, which is more than any of the other numbers. If several values appear an equal and most frequent number of times, both values are considered the mode.

Other useful indicators include range and outliers. The **range** is the difference between the highest and the lowest number in a data set. For example, the range of the set {16, 19, 19, 25, 27, 29, 75} is 75 – 16 = 59. **Outliers**, or data points that are much different from other data points, should be noted as they can skew the central tendency. In the data set {16, 19, 19, 25, 27, 29, 75}, the value 75 is far outside the other values and raises the value of the mean. Without the outlier, the mean is much closer to the other data points.

CHECK YOUR UNDERSTANDING

Why should paraprofessionals understand the importance of outliers when looking at student data?

- $\frac{16 + 19 + 19 + 25 + 27 + 29 + 75}{7} = \frac{210}{7} = 30$
- $\frac{16 + 19 + 19 + 25 + 27 + 29}{6} = 22.5$

When a data distribution is symmetrical, the mean, median, and mode tend to be in the center of the data. Generally, the median is a better indicator of a central tendency if outliers are present to skew the mean. If a distribution is **skewed left** (outliers tend to be smaller numbers), typically the mean is less than the median, and the median is the best indicator. If the distribution is **skewed right** (outliers tend to be larger numbers), typically the mean is greater than the median, and again, the median is the best indicator. So, the mean tends to be pulled toward the longer "tails" of the data.

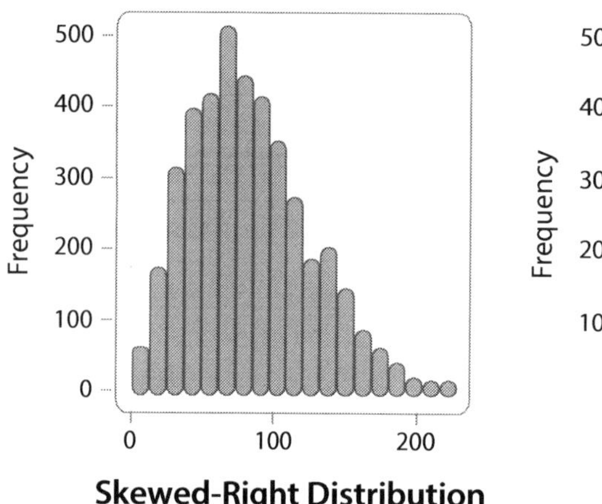

Figure 3.29. Skew

SAMPLE QUESTIONS

30) Ken has 6 grades in English class. Each grade is worth 100 points. Ken has a 92% average in English. If Ken's first five grades are 90, 100, 95, 83, and 87, what did Ken earn for the sixth grade?

A. 80

B. 92

C. 97

D. 100

31) What is the relationship between the mean and the median in a data set that is skewed right?

A. The mean is greater than the median.

B. The mean is less than the median.

C. The mean and median are equal.

D. The mean may be greater than, less than, or equal to the median.

DATA PRESENTATION

Data can be presented in a variety of ways. The most appropriate depends on the data being displayed.

Box plots (also called box-and-whisker plots) show data using the median, range, and outliers of a data set. They provide a helpful visual guide, showing how data is distributed around the median. In the example below, 81 is the median and the range is 100 – 0, or 100.

Figure 3.30. Box Plots

Bar graphs use bars of different lengths to compare data. The independent variable on a bar graph is grouped into categories such as months, flavors, or locations, and the dependent variable will be a quantity. Thus, comparing the length of bars provides a visual guide to the relative amounts in each category. **Double bar graphs** show more than one data set on the same set of axes.

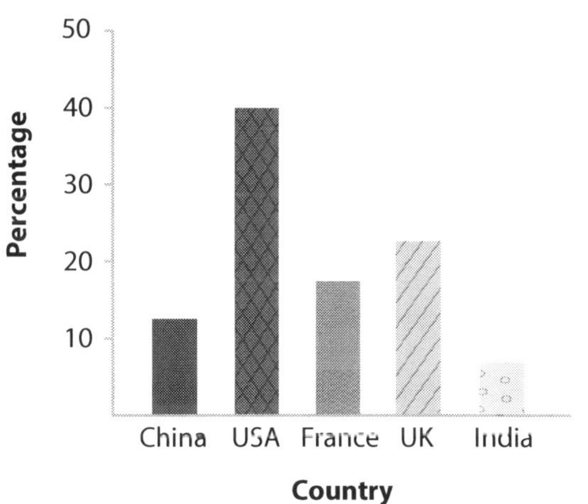

Figure 3.31. Bar Graph

Histograms similarly use bars to compare data, but the independent variable is a continuous variable that has been "binned" or divided into categories. For example, the time of day can be broken down into 8:00 a.m. to 12:00 p.m., 12:00 p.m. to 4:00 p.m., and so on. Usually (but not always), a gap is included between the bars of a bar graph but not a histogram.

Dot plots display the frequency of a value or event data graphically using dots, and thus can be used to observe the distribution of a data set. Typically, a value or

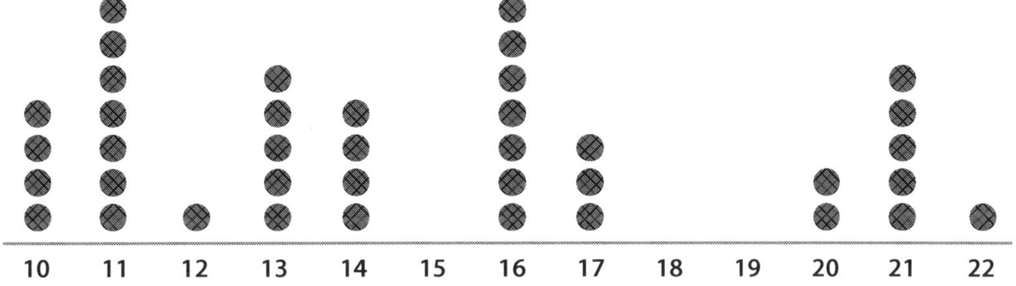

Figure 3.32. Dot Plot

category is listed on the *x*-axis, and the number of times that value appears in the data set is represented by a line of vertical dots. Dot plots make it easy to see which values occur most often.

Scatterplots use points to show relationships between two variables which can be plotted as coordinate points. One variable describes a position on the *x*-axis, and the other a point on the *y*-axis. Scatterplots can suggest relationships between variables. For example, both variables might increase, or one may increase when the other decreases.

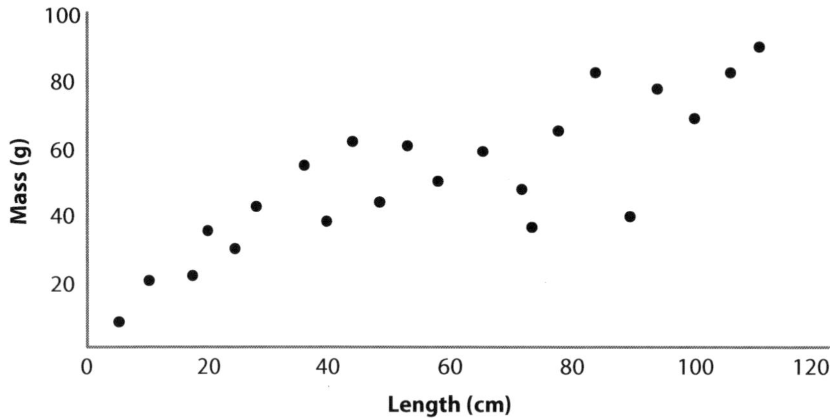

Figure 3.33. Scatterplot

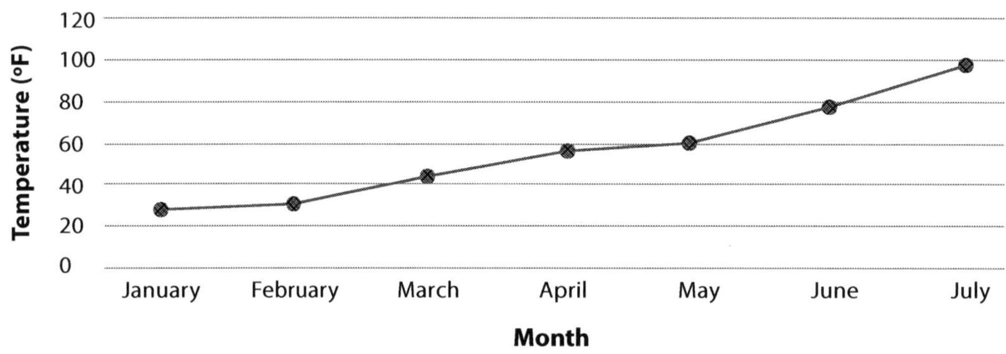

Figure 3.35. Line Graph

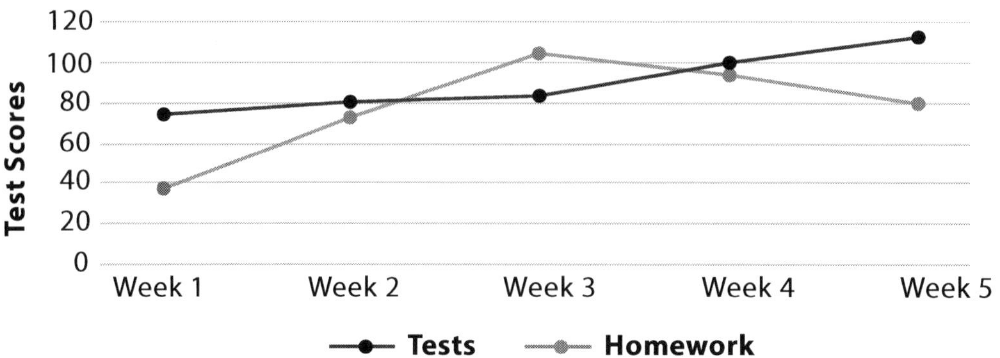

Figure 3.36. Double Line Graph

Line graphs show changes in data by connecting points on a scatterplot using a line. These graphs will often measure time on the *x*-axis and are used to show trends in the data, such as temperature changes over a day or school attendance throughout the year. **Double line graphs** present two sets of data on the same set of axes.

Circle graphs (also called pie charts) are used to show parts of a whole: the "pie" is the whole, and each "slice" represents a percentage or part of the whole.

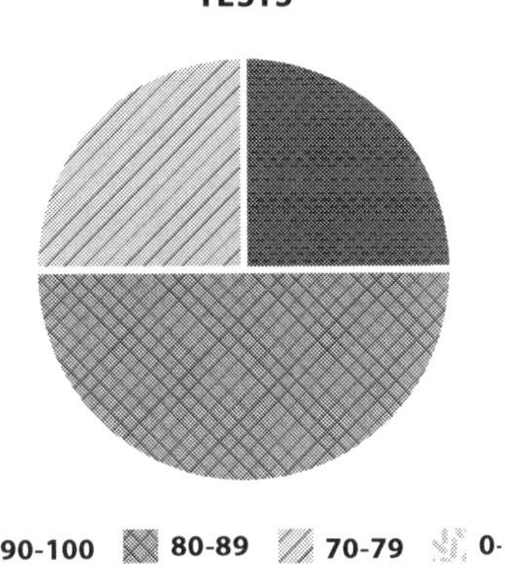

Figure 3.36. Circle Graph

SAMPLE QUESTION

32) The pie graph below shows how a state's government plans to spend its annual budget of $3 billion. How much more money does the state plan to spend on infrastructure than education?

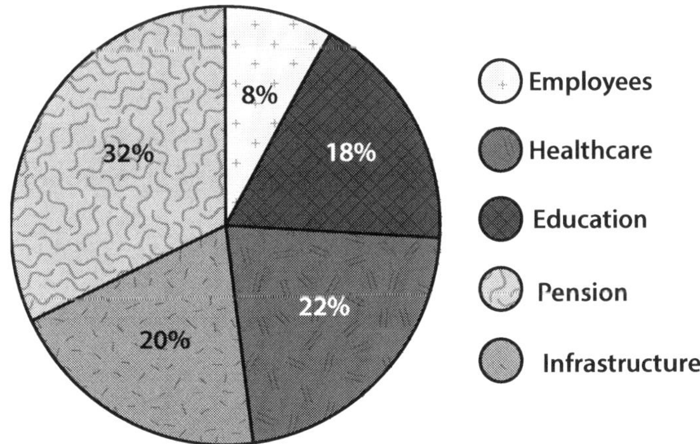

A. $60,000,000

B. $120,000,000

C. $300,000,000

D. $600,000,000

Answer Key

1) A. Incorrect. Students should grasp the concept of counting numbers before moving to negative numbers.

B. Incorrect. Pictures are a representation. Students should begin with concrete activities.

C. Incorrect. Numeral cards are abstract. Number cards are a representation.

D. **Correct.** Counters and toys are concrete objects.

2) **A.** **Correct.** Students are using the cubes to find different ways to make the number 7. The different ways can be listed on chart paper as number pairs that equal 7.

B. Incorrect. Students can subitize when they are able to quickly identify the number of items in a set without counting them.

C. Incorrect. Students must master conservation of numbers before they begin breaking specific numbers down into parts.

D. Incorrect. Students must master comparing numbers using the terms *greater*, *fewer*, *less*, and *more* before they begin breaking specific numbers into parts.

3) **A.** The number 3 is not irrational because it can be written as the fraction $\frac{3}{1}$.

4) **C.** If each student receives 2 notebooks, the teacher will need $16 \times 2 = 32$ notebooks. After handing out the notebooks, she will have $50 - 32 =$ **18** notebooks left.

5) A. Incorrect. This would be the correct answer if the student was not making an error. The question asks for the incorrect answer that the student would get if the error pattern continues.

B. Incorrect. This answer comes from the student adding ten to the ones column without reducing the tens column by one.

C. **Correct.** This answer follows the error pattern. Rather than regrouping, the student is confusing the minuend and the subtrahend in the ones column.

D. Incorrect. The answer adds instead of subtracts.

6) **C.** Write out the multiples for each number until reaching a number in both lists.

10: 10, 20, 30, 40, 50, **60**

12: 12, 24, 36, 48, **60**

7) **C.** Evaluate to find the expression with the greatest value.

$-4(3)(-2) = 24$

$-16 - 17 + 31 = -2$

$18 - 15 + 27 = \mathbf{30}$

$-20 + 10 + 10 = 0$

8) A. Incorrect. Solve inside the parentheses first, then multiply:

$2(200 - 8) = 2 \times 192 = 384$

B. Incorrect. Solve inside the parentheses first, then divide:

$(400 \div 4) \div 12 = 100 \div 12 = 8.333\ldots$

C. Incorrect. Solve inside the parentheses first, then add: $(216 \div 8) + (184 \div 8) = 27 + 23 = 50$

D. Correct. Solve inside the parentheses first, then add: $(216 \div 16) + (184 \div 16) = 13.5 + 11.5 = 25$

9) A. Incorrect. The associative property is a part of order of operations and must be understood to master it.

B. Incorrect. The associative property may help with simplifying two-step equations.

C. Correct. The associative property addresses grouping addition or multiplication problems. To understand the associative property, students should know how to add and multiply.

D. Incorrect. While some associate property problems may involve fractions, most will involve whole numbers.

10) C. Divide 1.3208 by 5.2.

$$\begin{array}{r} .254 \\ 52\overline{)13.208} \\ \underline{104} \\ 280 \\ \underline{260} \\ 208 \\ \underline{208} \\ 0 \end{array}$$

There is a **5** in the hundredths place.

11) A. Incorrect. 9,299 ones is not the correct answer because 9,299 ones = 9,299.

B. Incorrect. 903 tens is not the correct answer because 903 tens = 9, 030.

C. Correct. 93 hundreds is the correct answer because 93 hundreds = 9,300, and 9,300 is greater than the other answer choices.

D. Incorrect. 9 thousands is not the correct answer because 9 thousands = 9,000.

12) A. Correct. The 8 is in the thousands place. Because the value to the right of the 8 is less than 5, the 8 remains the same and all values to its right become zero. The result is 498,000.

13) A. Incorrect. Simplifying exponents is not a step in adding fractions.

B. Incorrect. Multiplying decimals is not related to adding fractions.

C. Correct. Being able to find the least common multiple helps a student find an equivalent fraction with a common denominator.

D. Incorrect. Adding fractions is not a multi-step equation.

14) B. 7 of 8 pizza slices are left after Carla takes 1, so $\frac{7}{8}$ of the pizza remains. 7 is the numerator of this fraction.

15) B. Convert each term to an improper fraction and multiple/divide left to right.

$1\frac{1}{2} = \frac{3}{2}$

$2\frac{2}{3} = \frac{8}{3}$

$1\frac{1}{4} = \frac{5}{4}$

$\left(1\frac{1}{2}\right)\left(2\frac{2}{3}\right) \div 1\frac{1}{4}$

$= \left(\frac{3}{2}\right)\left(\frac{8}{3}\right) \div \frac{5}{4}$

$= \frac{24}{6} \div \frac{5}{4}$

$= \frac{4}{1} \times \frac{4}{5} = \frac{16}{5} = \mathbf{3\frac{1}{5}}$

16) A. **Correct.** Equivalent fractions with common denominators must be used to add fractions. The LCM helps the student find the equivalent fraction.

B. Incorrect. Fractions can easily be added with unlike numerators, as long as they have common denominators.

C. Incorrect. Multiplying fractions does not require a common denominator.

D. Incorrect. Dividing fractions does not require a common denominator.

17) D. Set up a proportion and solve.

$\frac{8}{650} = \frac{12}{x}$

$12(650) = 8x$

$\mathbf{x = 975}$ **miles**

18) A. Substitute 5 for x.

$2(5) - 3 = 10 - 3 = 7$

19) D. The phase "gives away" describes subtraction, so after giving away 4 pieces of candy, Sawyer has $c - 4$ pieces left. The word "splits" describes division, so when she splits the remaining candy into two groups (one for her and one for her sister), she has $(c - 4) \div 2$ pieces.

20) A. Isolate the variable x on one side of the equation.

$5x - 4 = 3(8 + 3x)$

$5x - 4 = 24 + 9x$

$-4 - 24 = 9x - 5x$

$-28 = 4x$

$-\frac{28}{4} = \frac{4x}{4}$

$\mathbf{x = -7}$

21) A. Incorrect. Partner work is great, but this activity is abstract.

B. Incorrect. Solving problems is abstract and should come after the mathematical concept has been learned using concrete objects.

C. Incorrect. This lesson is a great way to incorporate partner work with representational materials, but begin teaching the concept with concrete objects.

D. **Correct.** Using concrete objects will help students obtain a conceptual understanding of the mathematical principles behind solving equations.

22) D. Plug in each set of values and determine if the inequality is true.

$2(0) + 0 \leq -10$ FALSE

$2(10) + 2 \leq -10$ FALSE

$2(10) + 10 \leq -10$ FALSE

$2(-10) + (-10) \leq -10$ **TRUE**

23) A. $4.25 \text{ km}\left(\frac{1000 \text{ m}}{1 \text{ km}}\right) = \mathbf{4250 \text{ m}}$

B. $\frac{8 \text{ m}^2}{\square} \times \frac{1000 \text{ mm}}{1 \text{ m}} \times \frac{1000 \text{ mm}}{1 \text{ m}}$

$= \mathbf{8{,}000{,}000 \text{ mm}^2}$

Since the units are *square* units (m^2), multiply by the conversion factor *twice,* so that both meters cancel (and $mm \times mm = mm^2$).

C. $12 \text{ ft}\left(\frac{12 \text{ in}}{1 \text{ ft}}\right) = \mathbf{144 \text{ in}}$

D. $23 \text{ m}\left(\frac{3.28 \text{ ft}}{1 \text{ m}}\right) = \mathbf{75.44 \text{ ft}}$

24) A. Incorrect. 15 mm is the length of line segment KL.

B. Correct. Line segment MN begins at 35 mm and ends at 70 mm, so 70 – 35 = 35 mm. The length of line segment KL is 15 mm. To find out how much longer MN is than KL, subtract, 35 mm – 15 mm = 20 mm.

C. Incorrect. 20 mm = 2 cm, not 2 mm.

D. Incorrect. 70 mm is where MN ends, 15 mm is the length of KL, and 70 – 15 = 55; however the distance between L and M is ignored.

25) A. Incorrect. This student tried to draw a larger angle by extending the rays farther from the vertex.

B. Incorrect. This student increased the size of the angle symbol but did not increase the size of the angle.

C. Incorrect. This student drew a smaller angle.

D. Correct. This student drew a larger angle.

26) C. Correct. Find the area of the square without the cut-outs; each side would be 12 mm long.

$12 \text{ mm} \times 12 \text{ mm} = 144 \text{ mm}^2$

Next, find the area of the cutouts.

$2 \text{ mm} \times 2 \text{ mm} = 4 \text{ mm}^2$

$4 \times 4 \text{ mm}^2 = 16 \text{ mm}^2$

Finally, subtract the total area of the four cut-outs from the total area of the square without the cut-outs.

$144 - 16 = 128 \text{ mm}^2$

27) A. Incorrect. To find the perimeter, the sides should be added, not multiplied.

B. Incorrect. Jack is calculating the area of the triangle.

C. Correct. Perimeter is found by adding all sides of a shape.

D. Incorrect. Matthew seems to be attempting to calculate the area, but should not be using the hypotenuse of the triangle.

28) A. Correct. A pyramid has 4 triangular faces and 1 square face.

B. Incorrect. There are no triangular faces on a cube.

C. Incorrect. There are no triangular faces on a rectangular prism.

D. Incorrect. There are no triangular faces on a cylinder.

29) B. Starting at the origin, move 5 units to the left, and then up 2 units.

30) C. If Ken has six scores that average 92%, his total number of points earned is found by multiplying the average by the number of scores:

$92 \times 6 = 552$

To find how many points he earned on the sixth test, subtract the sum of the other scores from 552:

$90 + 100 + 95 + 83 + 87 = 455$

$552 - 455 = 97$

31) A. If the data is skewed right, the set includes extreme values that are to the right, or high. The median is unaffected by these high values, but the mean includes these high values and would therefore be greater.

32) A. Find the amount the state will spend on infrastructure and education, and then find the difference.

$infrastructure = 0.2(3{,}000{,}000{,}000) = 600{,}000{,}000$

$education = 0.18(3{,}000{,}000{,}000) = 540{,}000{,}000$

$600{,}000{,}000 - 540{,}000{,}000 =$ **$60,000,000**

Writing Skills and Knowledge

On the ParaPro, Writing Skills and Knowledge questions ask about the basic rules of grammar. The first step in getting ready for this section of the test is to review the parts of speech and the rules that accompany them. Some of the topics you might see include:

- identifying parts of speech in a sentence
- matching pronouns with their antecedents
- matching verbs with their subjects
- ensuring that verbs are in the correct tense
- spelling irregular, hyphenated, and commonly misspelled words
- using correct capitalization
- distinguishing between types of sentences
- correcting sentence structure

Nouns and Pronouns

Nouns are people, places, or things. The subject of a sentence is typically a noun. For example, in the sentence "The hospital was very clean," the subject, *hospital*, is a noun; it is a place. **Pronouns** stand in for nouns and can be used to make sentences sound less repetitive. Take the sentence, "Sam stayed home from school because Sam was not feeling well." The word *Sam* appears twice in the same sentence. Instead, you can use the pronoun *he* to stand in for *Sam* and say, "Sam stayed home from school because he was not feeling well."

HELPFUL HINT

SINGULAR PRONOUNS

- I, me, my, mine
- you, your, yours
- he, him, his
- she, her, hers
- it, its

PLURAL PRONOUNS

- we, us, our, ours
- they, them, their, theirs

Because pronouns take the place of nouns, they need to agree both in number and gender with the noun they replace. So, a plural noun needs a plural pronoun, and a noun referring to something feminine needs a feminine pronoun. In the first sentence in this paragraph, for example, the plural pronoun *they* replaced the plural noun *pronouns*.

> Wrong: If a student forgets their homework, they will not receive a grade.

> Correct: If a student forgets his or her homework, he or she will not receive a grade.

Student is a singular noun, but *their* and *they* are plural pronouns. So, the first sentence is incorrect. To correct it, use the singular pronoun *his* or *her* or *he* or *she*.

> Wrong: Everybody will receive their paychecks promptly.

> Correct: Everybody will receive his or her paycheck promptly.

Everybody is a singular noun, but *their* is a plural pronoun. So, this sentence is incorrect. To correct it, use the singular pronoun *his* or *her*.

> Wrong: When nurses scrub in to surgery, you should wash your hands.

> Correct: When nurses scrub in to surgery, they should wash their hands.

This sentence begins in third-person perspective and then switches to second-person perspective. So, this sentence is incorrect. To correct it, use a third-person pronoun in the second clause.

> Wrong: After the teacher spoke to the student, she realized her mistake.

> Correct: After Mr. White spoke to his student, she realized her mistake. (*She* and *her* refer to the student.)

> Correct: After speaking to the student, the teacher realized her own mistake. (*Her* refers to the teacher.)

This sentence refers to a teacher and a student. But whom does *she* refer to, the teacher or the student? To eliminate the ambiguity, use specific names or state more specifically who made the mistake.

SAMPLE QUESTIONS

1) I have lived in Minnesota since August, but I still don't own a warm coat or gloves.

Which of the following lists includes all the nouns in the sentence?

A. coat, gloves
B. I, coat, gloves
C. Minnesota, August, coat, gloves
D. I, Minnesota, August, warm, coat, gloves

2) **In which of the following sentences do the nouns and pronouns not agree?**
A. After we walked inside, we took off our hats and shoes and hung them in the closet.
B. The members of the band should leave her instruments in the rehearsal room.
C. The janitor on duty should rinse out his or her mop before leaving for the day.
D. When you see someone in trouble, you should always try to help them.

VERBS

A **verb** is the action of a sentence: it describes what the subject of the sentence is or is doing. Verbs must match the subject of the sentence in person and number, and must be in the proper tense—past, present, or future.

Person describes the relationship of the speaker to the subject of the sentence: first (I, we), second (you), and third (he, she, it, they). *Number* refers to whether the subject of the sentence is singular or plural. Verbs are conjugated to match the person and number of the subject.

Table 4.1. Conjugating Verbs for Person

Person	Singular	Plural
First	I jump	we jump
Second	you jump	you jump
Third	he/she/it jumps	they jump

Wrong: The cat chase the ball while the dogs runs in the yard.

Correct: The cat chases the ball while the dogs run in the yard.

Cat is singular, so it takes a singular verb (which confusingly ends with an *s*); *dogs* is plural, so it needs a plural verb.

Wrong: The cars that had been recalled by the manufacturer was returned within a few months.

> Correct: The cars that had been recalled by the manufacturer were returned within a few months.

Sometimes, the subject and verb are separated by clauses or phrases. Here, the subject *cars* is separated from the verb by the relatively long phrase "that had been recalled by the manufacturer," making it more difficult to determine how to correctly conjugate the verb.

> Correct: The doctor and nurse work in the hospital.

> Correct: Neither the nurse nor her boss was scheduled to take a vacation.

> Correct: Either the patient or her parents need to sign the release forms.

When the subject contains two or more nouns connected by *and*, that subject becomes plural and requires a plural verb. Singular subjects joined by *or, either/or, neither/nor*, or *not only/but also* remain singular; when these words join plural and singular subjects, the verb should match the closest subject.

> HELPFUL HINT
>
> Think of the subject and the verb as sharing a single *s*. If the subject ends with an *s*, the verb should not, and vice versa.

Finally, verbs must be conjugated for tense, which shows when the action happened. Some conjugations include helping verbs like *was*, *have*, *have been*, and *will have been*.

Table 4.2. Verb Tenses

Tense	Past	Present	Future
Simple	I gave her a gift yesterday.	I give her a gift every day.	I will give her a gift on her birthday.
Continuous	I was giving her a gift when you got here.	I am giving her a gift; come in!	I will be giving her a gift at dinner.
Perfect	I had given her a gift before you got there.	I have given her a gift already.	I will have given her a gift by midnight.
Perfect continuous	Her friends had been giving her gifts all night when I arrived.	I have been giving her gifts every year for nine years.	I will have been giving her gifts on holidays for ten years next year.

Tense must also be consistent throughout the sentence and the passage. For example, the sentence *I was baking cookies and eat some dough* sounds strange. That is because the two verbs, *was baking* and *eat*, are in different tenses. *Was baking* occurred in the past; *eat*, on the other hand, occurs in the present. To make them consistent, change *eat* to *ate*.

> Wrong: Because it will rain during the party last night, we had to move the tables inside.

> Correct: Because it rained during the party last night, we had to move the tables inside.

All the verb tenses in a sentence need to agree both with each other and with the other information in the sentence. In the first sentence above, the tense does not match the other information in the sentence: *last night* indicates the past (*rained*), not the future (*will rain*).

> HELPFUL HINT
>
> If the subject is separated from the verb, cross out the phrases between them to make conjugation easier.

SAMPLE QUESTIONS

3) **Which of the following sentences contains an incorrectly conjugated verb?**
   A. The brother and sister runs very fast.
   B. Neither Anne nor Suzy likes the soup.
   C. The mother and father love their new baby.
   D. Either Jack or Jill will pick up the pizza.

4) **Which of the following sentences contains an incorrect verb tense?**
   A. After the show ended, we drove to the restaurant for dinner.
   B. Anne went to the mall before she headed home.
   C. Johnny went to the movies after he cleans the kitchen.
   D. Before the alarm sounded, smoke filled the cafeteria.

ADJECTIVES AND ADVERBS

Adjectives provide more information about a noun in a sentence. Take the sentence, "The boy hit the ball." If you want your readers to know more about the noun *boy*, you could use an adjective to describe him: *the little boy, the young boy, the tall boy.*

Adverbs and adjectives are similar because they provide more information about a part of a sentence. However, adverbs do not describe nouns—that's an adjective's job. Instead, adverbs describe verbs, adjectives, and even other adverbs. For example, in the sentence "The doctor had recently hired a new employee," the adverb *recently* tells us more about how the action *hired* took place.

Adjectives, adverbs, and **modifying phrases** (groups of words that together modify another word) should be placed as close as possible to the word they modify. Separating words from their modifiers can create incorrect or confusing sentences.

> Wrong: Running through the hall, the bell rang and the student knew she was late.

> Correct: Running through the hall, the student heard the bell ring and knew she was late.

The phrase *running through the hall* should be placed next to *student*, the noun it modifies.

The suffixes –er and –est are often used to modify adjectives when a sentence is making a comparison. The suffix –er is used when comparing two things, and the suffix –est is used when comparing more than two.

> Anne is taller than Steve, but Steve is more coordinated.

> Of the five brothers, Billy is the funniest, and Alex is the most intelligent.

Adjectives longer than two syllables are compared using *more* (for two things) or *most* (for three or more things).

> Wrong: Of my two friends, Clara is the smartest.

> Correct: Of my two friends, Clara is smarter.

More and *most* should NOT be used in conjunction with –er and –est endings.

> Wrong: My most warmest sweater is made of wool.

> Correct: My warmest sweater is made of wool.

SAMPLE QUESTIONS

5) **The new chef carefully stirred the boiling soup and then lowered the heat. Which of the following lists includes all the adjectives in the sentence?**

   A. new, boiling
   B. new, carefully, boiling
   C. new, carefully, boiling, heat
   D. new, carefully, boiling, lowered, heat

6) **Which of the following sentences contains an adjective error?**

   A. The new red car was faster than the old blue car.
   B. Reggie's apartment is in the tallest building on the block.
   C. The slice of cake was tastier than the brownie.
   D. Of the four speeches, Jerry's was the most long.

OTHER PARTS OF SPEECH

Prepositions express the location of a noun or pronoun in relation to other words and phrases described in a sentence. For example, in the sentence "The nurse parked her car in a parking garage," the preposition *in* describes the position of the car in relation to the garage. Together, the preposition and the noun that follow it are called a **prepositional phrase**. In this example, the prepositional phrase is *in a parking garage*.

> HELPFUL HINT
>
> An independent (or main) clause can stand alone as its own sentence. A dependent (or subordinate) clause must be attached to an independent clause to make a complete sentence.

Conjunctions connect words, phrases, and clauses. The conjunctions summarized in the acronym FANBOYS—For, And, Nor, But, Or, Yet, So—are called **coordinating conjunctions** and are used to join **independent clauses** (clauses that can stand alone as a complete sentence). For example, in the following sentence, the conjunction *and* joins together two independent clauses:

> The nurse prepared the patient for surgery, <u>and</u> the doctor performed the surgery.

Other conjunctions, like *although*, *because*, and *if*, join together an independent and **dependent clause** (which cannot stand on its own). Take the following sentence:

> She had to ride the subway <u>because her car was broken</u>.

The clause *because her car was broken* cannot stand on its own.

Interjections, like *wow* and *hey*, express emotion and are most commonly used in conversation and casual writing.

SAMPLE QUESTIONS

Choose the word that best completes the sentence.

7) Her love _____ blueberry muffins kept her coming back to the bakery every week.

A. to

B. with

C. of

D. about

8) Christine left her house early on Monday morning, _____ she was still late for work.

A. but

B. and

C. for

D. or

Sentence Structure

Phrases

Understanding subjects and predicates is key to understanding what a phrase is. The **subject** is what the sentence is about; the **predicate** contains the verb and its modifiers.

The nurse at the front desk will answer any questions you have.

Subject: the nurse at the front desk

Predicate: will answer any questions you have

A **phrase** is a group of words that communicates only part of an idea because it lacks either a subject or a predicate. Phrases are categorized based on the main word in the phrase. A **prepositional phrase** begins with a preposition and ends with an object of the preposition, a **verb phrase** is composed of the main verb along with any helping verbs, and a **noun phrase** consists of a noun and its modifiers.

Prepositional phrase: The dog is hiding under the porch.

Verb phrase: The chef wanted to cook a different dish.

Noun phrase: The big red barn rests beside the vacant chicken house.

SAMPLE QUESTION

9) **Identify the type of phrase underlined in the following sentence:**

The experienced paraprofessional worked independently with the eager students.

A. prepositional phrase

B. noun phrase

C. verb phrase

D. verbal phrase

Clauses

Clauses contain both a subject and a predicate. They can be either independent or dependent. An **independent** (or main) **clause** can stand alone as its own sentence.

The dog ate her homework.

Dependent (or subordinate) clauses cannot stand alone as their own sentences. They start with a subordinating conjunction, relative pronoun, or relative adjective, which will make them sound incomplete.

Because the dog ate her homework

A sentence can be classified as simple, compound, complex, or compound-complex based on the type and number of clauses it has.

Table 4.3. Types of Clauses

Sentence type	Number of independent clauses	Number of dependent clauses
simple	1	0
compound	2 or more	0
complex	1	1 or more
compound-complex	2 or more	1 or more

A **simple sentence** consists of one independent clause. Because there are no dependent clauses in a simple sentence, it can be a two-word sentence, with one word being the subject and the other word being the verb, such as *I ran*. However, a simple sentence can also contain prepositions, adjectives, and adverbs. Even though these additions can extend the length of a simple sentence, it is still considered a simple sentence as long as it does not contain any dependent clauses.

San Francisco in the springtime is one of my favorite places to visit.

Although the sentence is lengthy, it is simple because it contains only one subject and one verb (*San Francisco* and *is*), modified by additional phrases.

HELPFUL HINT

On the test you will have to both identify and construct different kinds of sentences.

Compound sentences have two or more independent clauses and no dependent clauses. Usually a comma and a coordinating conjunction (the FANBOYS: *For, And, Nor, But, Or, Yet,* and *So*) join the independent clauses, though semicolons can be used as well. The sentence "My computer broke, so I took it to be repaired" is compound.

The game was canceled, but we will still practice on Saturday.

This sentence is made up of two independent clauses joined by a conjunction (*but*), so it is compound.

HELPFUL HINT

Can you write a simple, compound, complex, and compound-complex sentence using the same independent clause?

Complex sentences have one independent clause and at least one dependent clause. In the complex sentence "If you lie down with dogs, you'll wake up with fleas," the first clause is dependent (because of the subordinating conjunction *if*), and the second is independent.

> I love listening to the radio in the car because I can sing along as loud as I want.

The sentence has one independent clause (*I love...car*) and one dependent (*because I...want*), so it is complex.

Compound-complex sentences have two or more independent clauses and at least one dependent clause. For example, the sentence *Even though David was a vegetarian, he went with his friends to steakhouses, but he focused on the conversation instead of the food*, is compound-complex.

> I wanted to get a dog, but I have a fish because my roommate is allergic to pet dander.

This sentence has three clauses: two independent (*I wanted...dog* and *I have a fish*) and one dependent (*because my...dander*), so it is compound-complex.

SAMPLE QUESTIONS

10) Which of the following choices is a simple sentence?

A. Elsa drove while Erica navigated.

B. Betty ordered a fruit salad, and Sue ordered eggs.

C. Because she was late, Jenny ran down the hall.

D. John ate breakfast with his mother, brother, and father.

11) Which of the following sentences is a compound-complex sentence?

A. While they were at the game, Anne cheered for the home team, but Harvey rooted for the underdogs.

B. The rain flooded all of the driveway, some of the yard, and even part of the sidewalk across the street.

C. After everyone finished the test, Mr. Brown passed a bowl of candy around the classroom.

D. All the flowers in the front yard are in bloom, and the trees around the house are lush and green.

PUNCTUATION

The basic rules for using the major punctuation marks are given in the table below.

Table 4.4. Using Punctuation

Punctuation	Purpose	Example
period	ending sentences	Periods go at the end of complete sentences.
question mark	ending questions	What's the best way to end a sentence?

Punctuation	Purpose	Example
exclamation point	ending sentences that show extreme emotion	I'll never understand how to use commas!
comma	joining two independent clauses (always with a coordinating conjunction)	Commas can be used to join clauses, but they must always be followed by a coordinating conjunction.
	setting apart introductory and nonessential words and phrases	Commas, when used properly, set apart extra information in a sentence.
	separating items in a list	My favorite punctuation marks include the colon, semicolon, and period.
semicolon	joining together two independent clauses (never used with a conjunction)	I love exclamation points; they make sentences seem so exciting!
colon	introducing a list, explanation, or definition	When I see a colon I know what to expect: more information.
apostrophe	forming contractions	It's amazing how many people can't use apostrophes correctly.
	showing possession	Parentheses are my sister's favorite punctuation; she finds commas' rules confusing.
quotation marks	indicating a direct quote	I said to her, "Tell me more about parentheses."

SAMPLE QUESTIONS

12) Which of the following sentences contains an error in punctuation?

A. I love apple pie! John exclaimed with a smile.

B. Jennifer loves Adam's new haircut.

C. Billy went to the store; he bought bread, milk, and cheese.

D. Alexandra hates raisins, but she loves chocolate chips.

13) Sam, why don't you come with us for dinner_

Which punctuation mark correctly completes the sentence?

A. .

B. ?

C. ;

D. :

Capitalization

Capitalization questions will ask you to spot errors in capitalization within a phrase or sentence. Below are the most important rules for capitalization you are likely to see on the test.

The first word of a sentence is always capitalized.

> We will be having dinner at a new restaurant tonight.

The first letter of a proper noun is always capitalized.

> We're going to Chicago on Wednesday.

Titles are capitalized if they precede the name they modify.

> Joe Biden, the vice president, met with President Obama.

Months are capitalized, but not the names of the seasons.

> Snow fell in March even though winter was over.

The names of major holidays should be capitalized. The word *day* is only capitalized if it is part of the holiday's name.

> We always go to a parade on Memorial Day, but Christmas day we stay home.

The names of specific places should always be capitalized. General location terms are not capitalized.

> We're going to San Francisco next weekend so I can see the ocean.

Titles for relatives should be capitalized when they precede a name, but not when they stand alone.

> Fred, my uncle, will make fried chicken, and Aunt Betty is going to make spaghetti.

SAMPLE QUESTION

14) Which of the following sentences contains an error in capitalization?

A. My two brothers are going to New Orleans for Mardi Gras.

B. On Friday we voted to elect a new class president.

C. Janet wants to go to Mexico this Spring.

D. Peter complimented the chef on his cooking.

SPELLING

The ParaPro will test you on spelling, so it is good to familiarize yourself with commonly misspelled words and special spelling rules. The test questions will ask you to either find a misspelled word in a sentence or identify words that don't follow standard spelling rules.

SPECIAL SPELLING RULES

- *i* comes before *e* except after *c*

  belief, thief, receive, ceiling

- Double a final consonant when adding suffixes if the consonant is preceded by a single vowel.

  run → running

  admit → admittance

- Drop the final vowel when adding a suffix.

  sue → suing

  observe → observance

- Change the final *y* to an *i* when adding a suffix.

  lazy → laziest

  tidy → tidily

Regular nouns are made plural by adding *s*. Irregular nouns can follow many different rules for pluralization, which are summarized in the table below.

Table 4.5. Irregular Plural Nouns

Ends with . . .	**Make it plural by . . .**	**Example**
y	changing *y* to *i* and adding *–es*	baby → babies
f	changing *f* to *v* and adding *–es*	leaf → leaves
fe	changing *f* to *v* and adding *–s*	knife → knives
o	adding *–es*	potato → potatoes
us	changing *–us* to *–i*	nucleus → nuclei
Always the same	**Doesn't follow the rules**	
sheep	man → men	
deer	child → children	
fish	person → people	
moose	tooth → teeth	
pants	goose → geese	
binoculars	mouse → mice	
scissors	ox → oxen	

COMMONLY MISSPELLED WORDS

- accommodate
- across
- argument
- believe
- committee
- completely
- conscious
- discipline
- experience
- foreign
- government
- guarantee
- height
- immediately
- intelligence
- judgment
- knowledge
- license
- lightning
- lose
- maneuver
- misspell
- noticeable
- occasionally
- occurred
- opinion
- personnel
- piece
- possession
- receive
- separate
- successful
- technique
- tendency
- unanimous
- until
- usually
- vacuum
- whether
- which

SAMPLE QUESTION

15) Which of the following sentences contains a spelling error?

A. It was unusually warm that winter, so we didn't need to use our fireplace.

B. Our garden includes tomatos, squash, and carrots.

C. The local zoo will be opening a new exhibit that includes African elephants.

D. My sister is learning to speak a foreign language so she can travel abroad.

ANSWER KEY

1) A. Incorrect. *Minnesota* and *August* are also nouns.

B. Incorrect. *I* is a pronoun; *Minnesota* and *August* are nouns.

C. **Correct.** *Minnesota* and *August* are proper nouns, and *coat* and *gloves* are common nouns. *I* is a pronoun, and *warm* is an adjective that modifies *coat*.

D. Incorrect. *I* is a pronoun, and *warm* is an adjective.

2) A. Incorrect. In this sentence, *hats and shoes* and *them* are all plural; they agree.

B. **Correct.** *The members of the band* is plural (*members*), so it should be replaced by the plural pronoun *their* instead of the singular *her*.

C. Incorrect. *Janitor* is singular, so the singular pronouns *his or her* are correct.

D. Incorrect. *You* and *you* agree in person and number.

3) **A.** **Correct.** Choice A should read "The brother and sister run very fast." When the subject contains two or more nouns connected by and, the subject is plural and requires a plural verb.

B. Incorrect. Since both *Anne* and *Suzy* are singular subjects connected by *neither…nor*, the verb *likes* should be conjugated in the singular. The verb *likes* is correctly conjugated here.

C. Incorrect. The verb *love* is conjugated correctly in the plural, because *mother and father* is a plural compound subject.

D. Incorrect. *Jack* and *Jill* are each singular subjects connected by *either…or*, so the verb should be conjugated in the singular: *will pick up*.

4) A. Incorrect. The past-tense verb *drove* is appropriately used to indicate that the speakers carried out their action *after* an event (the completion of the show). It also makes sense that the verb *ended* is conjugated in the past tense, for the show is over before any other events in the sentence occur.

B. Incorrect. The verb *went* is correctly conjugated in the past tense, indicating that Anne's action occurred "*before* she headed home." Likewise, it makes sense that *headed* is conjugated in the past tense.

C. **Correct.** Choice C should read "Johnny will go to the movies after he cleans the kitchen." It does not make sense to say that Johnny does something in the past (*went to the movies*) after doing something in the present (*after he cleans*).

D. Incorrect. Since the smoke appeared "*before* the alarm sounded," its verb, *filled*, must be conjugated in the past tense. The verb *sounded* may be conjugated in the past tense as well.

5) **A.** **Correct.** *New* modifies the noun *chef*, and *boiling* modifies the noun *soup*.

B. Incorrect. *Carefully* is an adverb modifying the verb *stirred*.

C. Incorrect. *Heat* is a noun.

D. Incorrect. *Lowered* is a verb.

6) A. Incorrect. The adjectives in this sentence—*new, red, faster, old*, and *blue*—are all correctly written. Since there are only two cars, using the comparative in *faster* is correct.

B. Incorrect. The adjective *tallest* is correctly written here: the sentence implies that there are multiple buildings on the block, a reasonable assumption, so the superlative is correctly used.

C. Incorrect. The adjective *tastier* is correctly written in the comparative here, because there are only two items being compared: a slice of cake and a brownie.

D. **Correct.** This sentence should read, "Of the four speeches, Jerry's was the longest." The word *long* has only one syllable, so it should be modified with the suffix *–est*, not the word *most*.

7) A. Incorrect. *To* frequently indicates position; it does not make sense here.

B. Incorrect. *With* often implies a physical connection; it does not make sense here.

C. **Correct.** The correct preposition is *of*. The preposition *of* usually shows a relationship and may accompany a verb.

D. Incorrect. *About* is not idiomatically paired with *love* and is thus incorrect.

8) **A.** **Correct.** In this sentence, the conjunction is joining together two contrasting ideas, so the correct answer is *but*.

B. Incorrect. Since the ideas in each clause of the sentence contrast, the conjunction *and* is not appropriate here. *But* is a better choice to clearly show the reader that the outcome of Christine's situation was unexpected. Usually, leaving one's home early would result in arriving at a destination early, but not for Christine.

C. Incorrect. The conjunction *for* is used to indicate cause and effect; it frequently can be replaced by the word *because*. Therefore, it would not be correct in this sentence, where the ideas contrast. Christine did not leave for work early *because* she was late to work. In fact, the opposite outcome occurred: despite leaving early, she was late.

D. Incorrect. The conjunction *or* signifies alternatives. It would not make sense here.

9) **A.** **Correct.** The phrase is a prepositional phrase beginning with the preposition *with*. The preposition *with* modifies *the eager students*.

10) A. Incorrect. This sentence is a complex sentence because it contains a dependent clause (*while Erica navigated*) and an independent clause (*Jenny ran down the hall*).

B. Incorrect. This sentence is a compound sentence: two independent clauses are connected by a comma and the coordinating conjunction *and*.

C. Incorrect. This sentence is a complex sentence because it contains a dependent clause (*Because she was late*) and an independent clause (*Elsa drove*).

D. Correct. This is the only sentence that contains one independent clause with one subject (*John*) and one verb (*ate*).

11) A. Correct. This sentence is a compound-complex sentence because it contains two independent clauses and one dependent clause.

B. Incorrect. Despite its length, this sentence is a simple sentence because it contains only one independent clause, *The rain flooded all of the driveway*.

C. Incorrect. This is a complex sentence because it contains one dependent clause (*After everyone finished the test*) and one independent clause.

D. Incorrect. This is a compound sentence; it contains two independent clauses connected with a comma and the conjunction *and*.

12) A. Correct. Choice A should use quotation marks to set off a direct quote: *"I love apple pie!" John exclaimed with a smile.*

13) B. Correct. The sentence is a question, so it should end with a question mark.

14) A. Incorrect. *New Orleans* and *Mardi Gras* are capitalized because they are proper nouns, the names of a location and a holiday.

B. Incorrect. *Friday* is a proper noun—the name of a day—and should therefore be capitalized.

C. Correct. *Spring* is the name of a season and should not be capitalized.

D. Incorrect. No words should be capitalized in this sentence, except *Peter*, because it is a proper noun and begins the sentence.

15) A. Incorrect. This sentence has no spelling error.

B. Correct. *Tomatos* should be spelled *tomatoes*.

C. Incorrect. All the words in this sentence are spelled correctly.

D. Incorrect. No spelling errors appear in this sentence.

Application of Writing Skills and Knowledge to Classroom Instruction

Writing

Production of Written Texts

Beginning in elementary school, students learn how to write in a variety of genres (e.g., personal narrative, tall tales, correspondence, poetry, science fiction, short stories, essays, research papers) and styles (e.g., descriptive, narrative, expository, persuasive). Students continue to practice such writing as they progress through the grades. Teachers select writing tasks to correlate with content knowledge goals assigned to grade levels via district and state standards. Paraprofessionals assist students in the writing process using prewriting strategies, drafting, editing, and consulting reference materials.

Elementary students also need to learn that writing is a process that begins with an idea and ends with a final draft. The writing process is made up of five key stages: prewriting, drafting, revising/editing, rewriting, and publishing. This process allows students to experience writing as it takes place in the profession. It is a process that enables students to capture the inspiration of the initial idea and then carefully shape and polish that idea until it can best capture a reader's interest.

During the **prewriting** phase of the writing process, authors brainstorm ideas for writing by organizing them in charts, lists, or by other means. This organization of ideas is used to write the **first draft** of a writing piece.

During the next stage of the process, a writer reviews the first draft for coherence by identifying sections that need elaboration, correction, and/or reorganization. In the **editing** phase, the original draft is revised based on these observations and those of peer editors. It is only after the first draft has been carefully examined and rewritten that it is ready for an audience during the **publishing** phase of the writing process.

In the earliest grades, elementary school students are provided with open-ended opportunities to develop as writers through both collaborative and independent writing activities such as lists, names, thematic vocabulary, pages for class books, individual books, journal entries, and responses to daily writing prompts. In addition, they practice forming letters using tactile and paper/pencil materials. Writer's workshops, in which students peer review, edit, and share writing, allow students to learn the writing process in small groups under a teacher's guidance. Paraprofessionals assist teachers by providing guidance to student groups and individual support to students as needed during writer's workshops.

As students move upward through the grades, writing assignments become more structured, and students learn the characteristics and conventions of writing using different forms, structures, and literary devices. As with reading comprehension, teachers use a number of strategies and tools to guide students as they work to attain writing proficiency. **Graphic organizers** provide ways for students to organize their ideas and clarify thinking at the beginning of the writing process. Some examples are listed below:

> QUICK REVIEW
>
> A student has completed a first draft of an essay about the novel *Roll of Thunder, Hear My Cry*. What should their teacher ask them to do next?

- **Concept map**: Using boxes and/or circles and lines, students begin with a main idea and draw links to supporting ideas, adding additional links and cross-links as necessary.

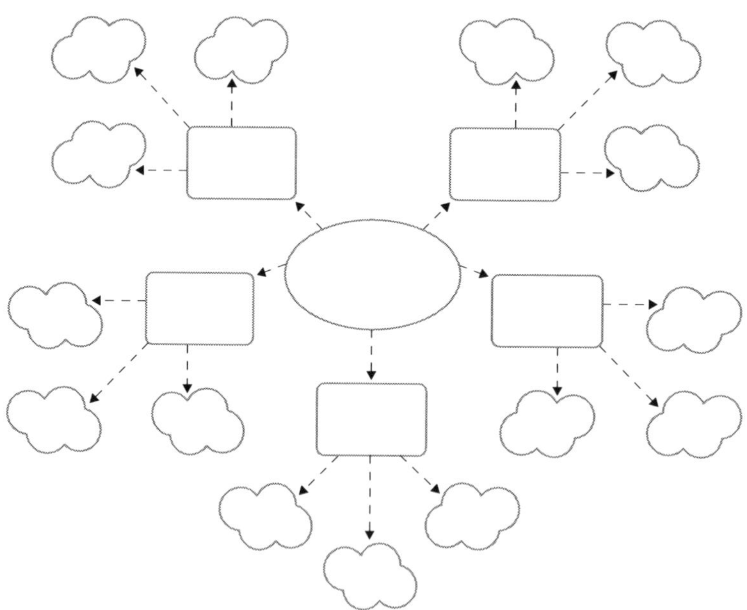

Figure 5.1. Concept Map

- **Story map**: Students brainstorm story elements and plan out the plot development of a story.
- **Lists**: Students brainstorm writing topics, story ideas, sensory words, rhyming words, alliterative words, etc.

- **Outlines**: Students create and revise formal working outlines as guides to writing expository essays and research papers.
- **Sequence maps**: Students draw or write events in the order they will occur in a text.
- **Beginning, middle, and end organizers**: Students plan the main structure of a writing piece by noting how it will begin (introduction), what is needed in the middle (body), and how it will end (conclusion).

Creative writing assignments provide opportunities for students to focus on concepts taught across the language arts curriculum. Reading and language concepts such as figurative language and word choice are naturally integrated into the writing process, as are literary elements such as character, setting, point of view, and plot.

In addition, **poetry** writing provides a wealth of opportunities for reinforcing concepts such as syllabification, spelling, vocabulary, parts of speech, and rhyming words. Some forms of poetry that may be accessible to students include the following:

- inquain: a five-line poem with a 2–4–6–8–2 syllable pattern
- haiku: a three-line poem with a 5–7–5 syllable pattern
- acrostic: a poem written for each letter in a word or phrase, reflecting its meaning
- diamante: a seven-line diamond-shaped poem requiring different parts of speech on each line
- quatrain: a four-line stanza with a rhyme scheme

SAMPLE QUESTIONS

1) **Which of the following elements shapes each paragraph in a writing task?**

    A. the thesis

    B. the topic sentence

    C. the drafting stage

    D. the outline

2) **A teacher has asked a paraprofessional to create a class-wide digital sampler to show parents the work her class has done during a unit on narrative writing. Which of the following phases in the authorship cycle is the teacher addressing?**

    A) brainstorming

    B) editing

    C) drafting

    D) publishing

Developmental Stages of Writing

Elementary school is where students establish a solid foundation of writing skills that lead to a lifelong ability to communicate ideas, opinions, experiences, and beliefs. Language arts teachers and paraprofessionals across the grades are tasked with building student understanding of writing styles, purposes, and practices.

Table 5.1. Developmental Stages of Writing

Stage	Age	Students in this stage...
Preconventional	3 – 5	▶ are aware that print conveys meaning but rely on pictures to communicate visually. ▶ include recognizable shapes and letters on drawings. ▶ can describe the significance of the objects in their drawings.
Emerging	4 – 6	▶ use pictures when drawing but may also label objects. ▶ can match some letters to sounds. ▶ copy print they see in their environment.
Developing	5 – 7	▶ write sentences and no longer rely mainly on pictures. ▶ attempt to use punctuation and capitalization. ▶ spell words based on sound.
Beginning	6 – 8	▶ write several related sentences on a topic. ▶ use word spacing, punctuation, and capitalization correctly. ▶ create writing that others can read.
Expanding	7 – 9	▶ organize sentences logically and use more complex sentence structures. ▶ spell high frequency words correctly. ▶ respond to guidance and criticism from others.
Bridging	8 – 10	▶ write about a particular topic with a clear beginning, middle, and end. ▶ begin to use paragraphs. ▶ consult outside resources (e.g., dictionaries).

Stage	Age	Students in this stage...
Fluent	9 – 11	▶ write both fiction and nonfiction with guidance. ▶ experiment with sentence length and complexity. ▶ edit for punctuation, spelling, and grammar.
Proficient	10 – 13	▶ write well-developed fiction and nonfiction. ▶ use transitional sentences and descriptive language. ▶ edit for organization and style.
Connecting	11 – 14	▶ write in a number of different genres. ▶ develop a personal voice when writing. ▶ use complex punctuation.
Independent	13 and older	▶ explore topics in depth in fiction and nonfiction. ▶ incorporate literary devices in their writing. ▶ revise writing through multiple drafts.

Research to Build and Present Knowledge

Supporting students in doing **research** and preparing reports based on that research is a fundamental role of paraprofessionals. Beginning in the early grades, students learn how to use print and multimedia sources to find out information and develop presentations—visual, written, and spoken—to share what they learned. Students learn how to navigate text and digital features, formulate questions, locate information, evaluate sources for reliability, identify primary and secondary sources, take notes, and paraphrase to avoid plagiarism. The research process is approached in a series of clear, focused, and manageable steps over a specified duration.

As students grow as writers, they learn how to cite sources to support their ideas in research papers. The research paper is an expository essay that contains references to outside materials that legitimize claims made in the essay. Students learn to **paraphrase** supporting information, or briefly restate it in their own words, in order to avoid **plagiarism**, the intentional copying and credit-taking of another person's work. They also learn to include **citations** that name original sources of new information and are taught how to differentiate between primary sources, secondary sources, reliable sources, and unreliable sources.

Primary sources are original materials representative of an event, experience, place, or time period. They are direct or firsthand accounts in the form of text, image, record, sound, or item. **Secondary sources** inform about events, experiences, places, or time periods, but the information is provided by someone who was not directly involved and who used primary sources to discuss the material.

Reliable sources are trustworthy materials that come from experts in the field of study. These sources have **credibility** because they include extensive bibliographies listing the sources used to support the information provided. Some examples of reliable sources are published books, articles in credible magazines, and research studies provided by educational institutions. **Unreliable sources** are untrustworthy materials from a person or institution that does not have the educational background, expertise, or evidence of legitimate sources to support a claim. Some examples of unreliable sources are self-published materials, studies done to sell products, and opinion pieces.

SAMPLE QUESTIONS

3) **Students have just been given a general overview of a research project due at the end of the semester. A paraprofessional might be asked to support students in which first task?**

   A. selecting a topic and locating some general information on the topic

   B. developing an outline listing the main idea and supporting details

   C. choosing reliable primary and secondary resources

   D. formulating an appropriate research question on a topic

4) **Which of the following is considered a reliable source for research about California?**

   A. a personal blog about living in California

   B. a research paper published by the state of California

   C. an advertisement for California real estate

   D. a letter to the editor about California roadways

Language

Within the contexts of reading comprehension and writing, teachers design instruction and select strategies and resources to develop students' understanding of Standard English conventions, vocabulary, and figurative language. This is especially true at the elementary levels. This section discusses several classroom tools. Paraprofessionals are an important source of instructional support and assist students in using these tools.

Editing checklists correlate to writing assignments; students use them to review and edit their work. These checklists include specific criteria for each assignment and bullet points such as "I used a capital at the beginning of each sentence," "I fixed words that do not look right," "Each sentence contains a noun and a verb," and "I used punctuation at the end of each sentence." Similarly, **peer editing checklists** are used by peers to edit classmates' writing. In a common three-part strategy, peers provide compliments, suggestions, and corrections.

In addition to checklists, visual aids can be used in instruction. **Word investigations** are graphic organizers used for in-depth word study. Students determine a word's definition, structural parts, part of speech, related words, and examples of the word used in context. Students may also use **figurative language graphic organizers** to find and interpret figurative language found in text. Students identify the type of figurative language used and use context to determine its meaning.

SAMPLE QUESTION

5) **A teacher is developing his students' reading vocabularies. Which strategy would the paraprofessional expect to support?**

A. having students peer edit each other's short stories

B. demonstrating how to use a dictionary

C. providing weekly opportunities for word investigations

D. brainstorming a list of words in a particular category

LISTENING AND SPEAKING

Listening and speaking are a child's pathway to literacy. Children typically enter elementary school with an ability to orally communicate ideas, experiences, and concepts. The role of paraprofessionals is to support teachers in creating an environment where students hone these skills for academic and social growth.

Language arts curriculum is designed to develop students' speaking and listening skills in conjunction with reading and writing skills, particularly at the elementary levels. Specific strategies are used to develop proficiency in the areas of active listening, oral presentation, and the use of **multimedia** (combined mediums of expression) to support speech. As in written assignments, paraprofessionals support students in preparing oral presentations and developing active listening skills.

PRESENTATION OF KNOWLEDGE AND IDEAS

In language arts classes, students learn strategies for listening and speaking that enhance their abilities to listen carefully, think critically, identify relevant information, articulate clearly, and use appropriate vocal cues and word choice. Students are tasked with communicating for a variety of purposes, audiences, and contexts and have opportunities to engage in active listening during discussions of text, topics, and community.

HELPFUL HINT

The organization of an oral presentation follows the same structure as that of a written essay: introduction, body, and conclusion. Similarly, the graphic organizers associated with writing can be used to develop an oral presentation.

As they do with other language arts skills that students are expected to acquire in elementary school, teachers chart the key elements of listening and speaking assignments and guide students through the process of preparing oral presentations in chunks or detailed steps. Across the duration of an oral presentation assignment, teachers cover the following material:

- **Delivery**: Posture, articulation, intonation, volume, eye contact, and expression
- **Organization**: A logical presentation structure with
  - a brief, attention-grabbing hook that captures the audience's interest (e.g., an amusing thought, an interesting prop, an intriguing fact, or a thought-provoking statement).
  - an introduction that states the topic and gives a brief overview of what will be covered.
  - a body of supporting evidence and/or details that correlate to and support the topic.
  - a conclusion that summarizes the presentation's main points.
- **Claims and Evidence**: Accuracy of content, strength of argument, use of source material, correlation between main idea and supporting details, logical progression of ideas, facts, and reasoned judgments
- **Audience Awareness**: Preparedness, appropriateness, and ability to hold audience attention
- **Visuals and/or Audio**: Supporting materials that reinforce content such as props, posters, digital media, photographs, music, etc.
- **Collaboration**: Creative, cohesive, and logical group presentations

Students are provided with opportunities to strengthen listening skills during classmates' oral presentations. They are tasked with providing **constructive feedback**—positively worded suggestions—derived from previously agreed-upon criteria for active listening: focus, respect, objectivity, and paraphrasing.

QUICK REVIEW

What challenges might a paraprofessional anticipate in supporting first-grade students preparing for an oral presentation research project?

SAMPLE QUESTIONS

6) **Which of the following might be a primary benefit of show-and-tell opportunities for students?**

   A. Students make decisions about what to share.

   B. Students rest at the end of a busy week.

   C. Students practice speaking in front of an audience.

   D. Students are rewarded for doing their homework.

7) **Which strategy is most typically used to grab the audience's attention at the beginning of an oral presentation?**

A. eye contact

B. a statement of topic

C. a loud voice

D. an engaging hook

8) **Students have been placed in small groups to prepare readers' theater presentations that they will perform for each other. How might each group best meet the needs of its audience?**

A. by reciting their lines in quiet voices during the performance

B. by passing around a script to read from during the performance

C. by using classroom materials as props during the performance

D. by skipping some parts of the story during the performance

Discussion and Collaboration

Learning is a social construct; social learning tools like collaboration and discussion are important to student learning. Discussion should be regularly incorporated into the curriculum from the earliest years.

The goals of discussion are twofold: to construct student understanding of content and to develop communication skills. To begin, students learn the elements of a good discussion. An essential skill is **active listening**: the process of demonstrating engagement through positive body language and then paraphrasing or summarizing of the speaker's content. Other discussion skills include active participation, asking clarifying questions, constructive disagreement, seeking out all voices, and supporting arguments with evidence.

Once parameters have been established, the teacher should lead the students in a discussion. In one tactic, **immersion**, all students participate in a discussion with little redirection or guidance. In contrast, in a **fishbowl** a small subset of students engages in discussion while the remaining students watch. In either case, the discussion should be followed by reflection, allowing students to analyze what was successful and unsuccessful about the discussion, and to find ways to improve their discussions in the future.

It is essential that teachers provide students ample opportunity to practice discussion, always followed by reflection. Through this process, students will learn to be respectful and considerate of others, to clearly express their own ideas orally, to listen and respond to the ideas of others, to ask clarifying questions and build on outside ideas, and to incorporate new ideas and perspectives into their own understanding.

The second form of social learning is **collaborative learning**. It is based on four general principles:

1. Students must be at the center of instruction.
2. Students learn more by working in groups.
3. Learning should focus on doing and interacting.
4. Students retain more information and gain more skills when addressing real-world problems.

Collaborative learning can take the form of peer learning or group learning. In **peer learning**, pairs or small groups of students discuss concepts or develop solutions to problems related to the content. With this method, students learn from each other, dispelling misconceptions and addressing misunderstandings. Informal practices include pair-share and talk-and-turns. More formal practices include case studies and debates. Many of the skills honed by discussions are also addressed in peer learning. Students must listen to each other, ask clarifying questions, and show mutual respect.

In **collaborative group work**, students typically work in larger groups or over a longer period of time. This approach is most often used with long-term projects in which students develop or pursue a particular question or problem, and then—working mostly independently of the teacher and paraprofessional—gather the needed information to solve it. For example, in a unit on the environment and sustainability, students might work in groups to reduce the classroom's energy use or waste creation. Students would then engage in research, develop plans, and test ideas, all working together without support from the paraprofessional.

When students work together to *do*, they learn important academic skills: formulating and answering questions, seeking help when needed, gathering and processing information, and evaluating and reflecting on the perspectives of others. Through this process, students develop self-management, oral communication, and leadership skills, as well as improve their understanding of the content.

In addition, collaborative learning builds student self-confidence, encouraging students to challenge themselves and to take greater risks. It prepares them for life beyond the classroom as they learn to navigate the challenges of working with others and to leverage the benefits of multiple minds.

SAMPLE QUESTION

9) **Which of the following best explains the primary purpose of a fishbowl activity?**

A. to assess individual student understanding after a group project

B. to allow students to observe and evaluate a discussion

C. to encourage students to collaborate in addressing misconceptions about an idea

D. to model for students how to develop effective discussion questions

ANSWER KEY

1) A. Incorrect. The thesis drives the entire essay.

B. **Correct.** The topic sentence for each paragraph introduces the idea that the paragraph will discuss.

C. Incorrect. The drafting stage addresses writing the entire document; it does not unify the content within each paragraph.

D. Incorrect. The outline drives the overall direction of the essay.

2) A) Incorrect. Brainstorming is the first phase in the authoring cycle where students generate ideas.

B) Incorrect. Editing involves revising work to make it more readable.

C) Incorrect. The students have already drafted the pieces in this vignette.

D) **Correct.** Publishing student work involves sharing it with others.

3) **A.** **Correct.** The first step in any research project is to select a topic of interest and acquire background knowledge about it. Once general information on a topic is understood, a relevant question can be formulated.

B. Incorrect. Prior to developing an outline, students need to select topics and formulate appropriate research questions.

C. Incorrect. Resources should be selected after a topic has been chosen and an appropriate research question has been formulated.

D. Incorrect. Research questions are best formulated after a topic has been selected and background knowledge acquired. Having a general idea of the issues surrounding a topic makes it easier to narrow the focus of a research project and formulate a relevant research question.

4) A. Incorrect. A personal blog is an unreliable source for research on a broad topic.

B. **Correct.** A published study by a government institution is a reliable research source.

C. Incorrect. Advertisements present biased information and are therefore unreliable sources of information.

D. Incorrect. Letters to the editors of newspapers typically include opinions, which are unreliable sources of information.

5) A. Incorrect. Peer editing is used during the revision stage of the writing process as a form of feedback before rewriting. Vocabulary development may occur, but it is not the focus of the task.

B. Incorrect. Learning how to use a dictionary is an important skill, but it does not necessarily increase vocabulary development over time in a systematic way.

C. **Correct.** Consistently providing opportunities for students to investigate words in-depth increases the probability that they will retain comprehension of the words over time.

D. Incorrect. Brainstorming a list of words in a particular category is a good prewriting strategy, but it is unlikely that it would significantly increase students' reading vocabularies because students are most likely suggesting words they already know.

6) A. Incorrect. While students do make decisions about what to share, this is secondary to the practice they receive speaking in front of an audience using proper delivery and audience awareness.

B. Incorrect. While students may enjoy show-and-tell, it is still an academic practice when the teacher applies expectations for speaking in front of an audience and active listening.

C. **Correct.** Opportunities for show-and-tell provide students with practice speaking in front of an audience. The audience members also receive practice exercising their active listening skills.

D. Incorrect. Show-and-tell benefits students by giving them practice speaking in front of an audience, which is an important skill, as opposed to an appropriate reward.

7) A. Incorrect. Eye contact is a strategy for maintaining an audience's interest during an oral presentation, but it is not the most effective strategy for gaining the audience's attention.

B. Incorrect. The introduction of an oral presentation must include a statement of topic, but it is best introduced by an engaging hook to gain the audience's attention.

C. Incorrect. Using a loud voice is not the best strategy for grabbing an audience's attention because it could be received as unprofessional or ill-mannered.

D. **Correct.** An engaging hook prior to the introduction of an oral presentation is typically used to grab the audience's attention.

8) A. Incorrect. Reciting lines in quiet voices makes it difficult for an audience to hear important details.

B. Incorrect. Reading from a shared script interrupts the flow of a performance and causes the audience to become restless.

C. **Correct.** Props add interesting visuals to a performance and reinforce comprehension.

D. Incorrect. Skipping some parts of a story is confusing to an audience.

9) A. Incorrect. Fishbowl discussions are not typically used for summative assessment.

B. **Correct.** In a fishbowl, half of the class observes only, allowing them to witness both positive and negative elements of a discussion.

C. Incorrect. While fishbowls can be used for this, it is not their primary purpose.

D. Incorrect. A fishbowl is an actual discussion, not preparation for one.

Practice Test

READING

Each of the questions or incomplete statements below is followed by four suggested answers or completions. Select the one that is best in each case.

1

A paraprofessional is quietly reading a book to Henry, a three-year-old student who did not fall asleep during nap time. As she reads, she is pointing to each word on the page. Which of the following is the paraprofessional trying to accomplish?

A. reinforce Henry's print awareness

B. keep a steady pace and rhythm as she reads

C. lull Henry to sleep

D. try to focus Henry's attention towards reading the words along with her

Question 2 is based on the following passage.

The Scream of Nature by Edvard Munch is one of the world's best known and most desirable artworks. While most people think of it as a single painting, the iconic creation actually has four different versions: two paintings and two pastels. In 2012, one of the pastels earned the fourth highest price paid for a painting at auction when it was sold for almost $120 million. The three others are not for sale; the Munch Museum in Oslo holds a painted version and a pastel version, while the National Gallery in Oslo holds the other painting. However, the desire to acquire them has been just as strong: in 1994 the National Gallery's version was stolen, and in 2004 the painting at the Munch Museum was stolen at gunpoint in the middle of the day. Both paintings were eventually recovered.

2

The primary purpose of the passage is to

A. describe the image depicted in *The Scream of Nature*.

B. explain the origin of the painting *The Scream of Nature*.

C. clarify the number of versions of *The Scream of Nature* that exist.

D. prove the high value of *The Scream of Nature*.

3

Which of the following is an example of an informational text?

A. poetry anthology

B. short story

C. novel

D. brochure

Question 4 is based on the following passage.

After World War I, powerful political and social forces pushed for a return to normalcy in the United States. The result was disengagement from the larger world and increased focus on American economic growth and personal enjoyment. Caught in the middle of this was a cache of American writers, raised on the values of the prewar world and frustrated with what they viewed as the superficiality and materialism of postwar American culture. Many of them, like Ernest Hemingway and F. Scott Fitzgerald, fled to Paris, where they became known as the "lost generation," creating a trove of literary works criticizing their home culture and delving into their own feelings of alienation.

4

In context, the word *cache* most nearly means

A. a group of the same type.

B. a majority segment.

C. an organization.

D. a dispersed number.

5

A paraprofessional notices a pre-kindergarten student, Rene, is pretending to read a book from the back cover to the front cover. Which of the following does Rene need more practice with?

A. phonemic awareness

B. phonological awareness

C. letter-sound correspondence

D. concepts of print

Question 6 is based on the following passage.

When the Spanish-American War broke out in 1898, the US Army was small and understaffed. President William McKinley called for 1,250 volunteers primarily from the Southwest to serve in the First US Volunteer Calvary. Eager to fight, the ranks were quickly filled by a diverse group of cowboys, gold prospectors, hunters, gamblers, Native Americans, veterans, police officers, and college students looking for an adventure. The officer corps was composed of veterans of the Civil War and the Indian Wars. With more volunteers than it could accept, the army set high standards: all the recruits had to be skilled on horseback and with guns. Consequently, they became known as the Rough Riders.

6

According to the passage, all the recruits were required to

A. have previously fought in a war.

B. be American citizens.

C. live in the Southwest.

D. ride a horse well.

7

Mark, a first-grade student, is sounding out the word *flat*. He sounds out the word "f-l-a-t." Which of the following is true about Mark?

A. He is lacking basic knowledge of the alphabetic principle.

B. He needs more practice with affixes.

C. He sounded out each letter individually versus the onset and rime.

D. He has a strong knowledge of consonant blends.

Question 8 is based on the following passage.

In 1953, doctors surgically removed the hippocampus of patient Henry Molaison in an attempt to stop his frequent seizures. Unexpectedly, he lost the ability to form new memories, leading to the biggest breakthrough in the science of memory. Molaison's long-term memory—of events more than a year before his surgery—was unchanged as was his ability to learn physical skills. From this, scientists learned that different types of memory are handled by different parts of the brain, with the hippocampus responsible for *episodic memory*, the short-term recall of events. They have since discovered that some memories are then channeled to the cortex, the outer layers of the brain that handle higher functions, where they are gradually integrated with related information to build lasting knowledge about our world.

8

The main idea of the passage is that

A. Molaison's surgery posed significant risk to the functioning of his brain.

B. short-term and long-term memory are stored in different parts of the brain.

C. long-term memory forms over a longer period than short-term memory.

D. memories of physical skills are processed differently than memories of events.

Question 9 is based on the following excerpt.

Tree Species by Ecosystem

Tropical Rain Forest: mahogany, Brazil nut, rubber tree, tualang, strangler figs

Tropical Dry Forest: palu, Ceylon ebony, governor's plum

Temperate Deciduous Forest: oak, maple, beech, elm, magnolia, sweet gum

Temperate Coniferous Forest: cedar, cypress, juniper, pine, spruce, redwood

9

According to the lists above, beech trees would be found in which ecosystem?

A. tropical rain forest

B. tropical dry forest

C. temperate deciduous forest

D. temperate coniferous forest

10

A paraprofessional, Mrs. Blake, wants to check a student's understanding of the first-person point of view. The student has recently read a story about a dinosaur. The story is told in the voice of the dinosaur. Which of the following questions would reveal to Mrs. Blake whether the student understands first-person point of view?

A. Why did the dinosaur want to become a ballerina?

B. What character told the story we just read?

C. Where did the story take place?

D. What did you like most about the story?

Question 11 is based on the following passage.

Between November 15 and December 21, 1864, Major General William Tecumseh Sherman marched Union troops from the recently captured city of Atlanta to the port of Savannah. The goal was not only to capture the port city and secure Georgia for the Union, but also to destroy the Confederacy's infrastructure and demoralize its people. Sherman and his troops destroyed rail lines and burned buildings and fields. They packed only twenty days' worth of rations, foraging for the rest of their supplies from farms along the way. By the time they reached Savannah, they had destroyed 300 miles of railroad, countless cotton gins and mills, seized 4,000 mules, 13,000 head of cattle, 9.5 million pounds of corn, and 10.5 million pounds of fodder. Sherman estimated his troops inflicted $100 million in damages.

11

It can be inferred from the passage that the Confederacy

A. strongly resisted the actions of Sherman's troops.

B. was greatly weakened by the destruction.

C. used Sherman's March as a rallying point.

D. was relatively unaffected by the march.

12

Which of the following best defines a story's plot?

A. sequence of events

B. climactic scene

C. problem that is resolved

D. time and place in which it is set

Question 13 is based on the following passage.

For thirteen years, a spacecraft called *Cassini* has been on an exploratory mission to Saturn. The spacecraft was designed not to return but to end its journey by diving into Saturn's atmosphere. This dramatic ending will provide scientists with unprecedented information about Saturn's atmosphere and its magnetic and gravitational fields. First, however, *Cassini* will pass Saturn's largest moon, Titan, where it will record any changes in Titan's curious methane lakes, gathering information about potential seasons on the planet-sized moon. Then it will pass through the unexplored region between Saturn itself and its famous rings. Scientists hope to learn how old the rings are and to directly examine the particles that make them up. It is likely that the spectacular end to *Cassini* will introduce new questions for future exploration.

13

According to the passage, scientists want to learn more about Titan's

A. gravity, based on examination of its magnetic field.

B. rings, based on the particles that compose them.

C. seasons, based on changes to its lakes.

D. age, based on analysis of its minerals and gases.

14

Which of the following concepts should be taught alongside phonics to ensure that students will be able to read quickly and fluently?

A. phonological awareness

B. sight word recognition

C. concepts of print

D. spelling

Question 15 is based on the following passage.

Researchers at the University of California, Berkeley, decided to tackle an age-old problem: why shoelaces come untied. They recorded the shoelaces of a volunteer walking on a treadmill by attaching devices to record the acceleration, or g-force, experienced by the knot. The results were surprising. A shoelace knot experiences more g-force from a person walking than any rollercoaster can generate. However, if the person simply stomped or swung their feet—the two movements that make up a walker's stride—the g-force was not enough to undo the knots. Researchers also found that while the knot loosened slowly at first, once it reached a certain laxness, it simply fell apart.

15

The author includes a comparison to rollercoasters in order to

A. illustrate the intensity of force experienced by the knots.

B. describe an experiment undertaken by researchers.

C. critique a main finding of the experiment.

D. provide further evidence to support the study's conclusion.

16

Which of the following statements is true about phonemic awareness?

A. It generally has to be explicitly taught.

B. It is natural and intuitive.

C. Most students will master it at the same rate.

D. Students do not need it to begin reading.

Question 17 is based on the following passage.

Archaeologists have discovered the oldest known specimens of bedbugs in a cave in Oregon where humans once lived. The three different species date back to between 5,000 and 11,000 years ago. The finding gives scientists a clue as to how bedbugs became human parasites. These bedbugs, like those that plague humans today, originated as bat parasites. Scientists hypothesize that it was the co-habitation of humans and bats in the caves that encouraged the bugs to begin feeding on the humans. The three species found in the Oregon caves are actually still around today, although they continue to prefer bats. Humans only lived seasonally in the Oregon cave system, however, which might explain why these insects did not fully transfer to human hosts like bedbugs elsewhere did.

17

With which of the following claims about bedbugs would the author most likely agree?

A. Ancient bedbugs did not easily transition to new animal hosts, slowing their evolution.

B. Modern bedbugs that prefer humans thrive better in areas with extensive light.

C. Bedbugs that prefer humans originated in caves that humans occupied year-round.

D. The transition to humans significantly accelerated the growth of bedbug populations.

Questions 18–20 are based on the figure below showing the inventory at Gigi's Diner below.

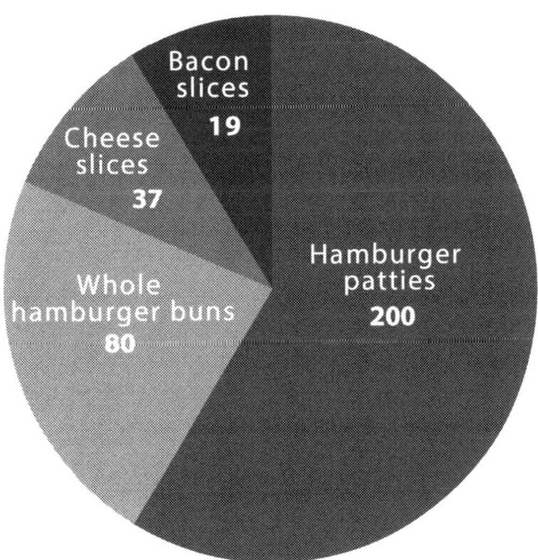

18

Which food does Gigi's have the least of?

A. bacon slices

B. cheese slices

C. hamburger buns

D. hamburger patties

19

According to the graph above, how many more hamburger buns does Gigi's need in order to make 200 hamburgers?

A. 120

B. 161

C. 181

D. 200

20

Which of the following is the number of hamburgers Gigi's could make if each burger includes one bacon slice and two cheese slices?

A. 18

B. 19

C. 39

D. 80

Question 21 is based on the following passage.

Tourists flock to Yellowstone National Park each year to view the geysers that bubble and erupt throughout it. What most of these tourists do not know is that these geysers are formed by a caldera, a hot crater in the earth's crust, that was created by a series of three eruptions of an ancient supervolcano. These eruptions, which began 2.1 million years ago, spewed between 1,000 to 2,450 cubic kilometers of volcanic matter at such a rate that the volcano's magma chamber collapsed, creating the craters.

21

The main idea of the passage is that

A. Yellowstone National Park is a popular tourist destination.

B. The geysers in Yellowstone National Park rest on a caldera in the earth's crust.

C. A supervolcano once sat in the area covered by Yellowstone National Park.

D. The earth's crust is weaker in Yellowstone National Park.

22

What question could a paraprofessional ask a pre-kindergarten student to help him identify the conflict in a story?

A. Who are the characters on this page?

B. How was the problem resolved?

C. Why was (character name) so mad?

D. Where did this story happen?

23

Which of the following pronouns is usually used with the second-person point of view?

A. he

B. I

C. us

D. you

24

Anna has just joined a teacher's first-grade class. She and her family just came to the school in Texas from China, and they speak very little English, especially Anna. Her home language is Mandarin, and its sounds are often very different from English sounds. The class is spending the bulk of its allotted reading time on phonics decoding and word-attack skills. Most of the class is working on spelling words with challenging consonant digraphs like –*ch*, –*sh*, and –*th*. How might the paraprofessional support Anna, who does not yet speak English fluently?

A. give her a book to read in Mandarin while the rest of the class is working on spelling

B. have her copy the spelling words instead of writing them independently

C. avoid any phonics support and focus on developing Anna's English vocabulary

D. assist Anna in an activity to familiarize her with basic English phonemes

Question 25 is based on the following passage.

The Battle of Little Bighorn, commonly called Custer's Last Stand, was a battle between the Lakota, the Northern Cheyenne, the Arapaho, and the Seventh Calvary Regiment of the US Army. Led by war leaders Crazy Horse and Chief Gall and the religious leader Sitting Bull, the allied tribes of the Plains Indians decisively defeated their US foes. Two hundred and sixty-eight US soldiers were killed, including General George Armstrong Custer, two of his brothers, his nephew, his brother-in-law, and six Indian scouts.

25

What is the main idea of this passage?

A. Most of General Custer's family died in the Battle of Little Bighorn.

B. The Battle of Little Bighorn was a significant victory for the Plains Indians.

C. The Seventh Calvary regiment was formed to fight Native American tribes.

D. Sitting Bull and George Custer were fierce enemies.

26

Which of the following is typical of a narrative written in first-person point of view?

A. The author is a minor secondary character.

B. The audience does not know what the protagonist is thinking.

C. The narrator, protagonist, and author are all the same person.

D. The author is an omniscient third person observer.

27

Which of the following is a popular list of sight words?

A. the lexile chart

B. the Flesch-Kincaid list

C. the Dolch list

D. the high-interest list

Question 28 is based on the following excerpt.

28

According to the excerpt from the psychology textbook index above, which of the following pages should a reader check first for information on short-term memory?

A. 316

B. 319

C. 333

D. 340

29

A paraprofessional is reading a story to a student to assist in an integrated unit on community leaders. The book is about a girl whose mother is running for mayor. About halfway through the book, the election happens. At this point, the paraprofessional stops on the page and asks, "What do you think is going to happen?" Which of the following skills is the paraprofessional helping the student practice?

A. building anticipation

B. making predictions

C. integrating curriculum

D. understanding character motivation

Question 30 is based on the following passage.

The cisco, a foot-long freshwater fish native to the Great Lakes, once thrived throughout the basin but had virtually disappeared by the 1950s. However, today fishermen are pulling them up by the net-load in Lake Michigan and Lake Ontario. It is highly unusual for a native species to revive, and the reason for the cisco's reemergence is even more unlikely. The cisco have an invasive species, quagga mussels, to thank for their return. Quagga mussels depleted nutrients in the lakes, harming other species highly dependent on these nutrients. Cisco, however, thrive in low-nutrient environments. As other species—many invasive—diminished, cisco flourished in their place.

30

It can be inferred from the passage that most invasive species

A. support the growth of native species.

B. do not impact the development of native species.

C. struggle to survive in their new environments.

D. cause the decline of native species.

Mathematics

Work the problem, and then choose the most correct answer.

1

How many digits are in the sum 951.4 + 98.908 + 1.053?

A. 4

B. 5

C. 6

D. 7

2

Ms. Evan's fourth-grade class is learning to add fractions. A student's work is shown below.

$\frac{2}{5} + \frac{1}{9} = \frac{3}{14}$

If the student uses the same strategy, what will his answer be to the problem below?

$\frac{1}{3} + \frac{1}{2} =$

A. $\frac{5}{6}$

B. $\frac{2}{5}$

C. 1

D. $\frac{1}{6}$

3

71 ÷ 31 is equal to

A. 0.341

B. 3.41

C. 34.1

D. 341

4

$1\frac{3}{4} + 2\frac{3}{8}$ is equal to

A. $3\frac{3}{4}$

B. $3\frac{7}{8}$

C. 4

D. $4\frac{1}{8}$

5

Ms. Chavez is helping her students develop strategies for solving basic equations. The work from one of her students in shown below.

$10y - 5 = 15$

$5y = 15$

$y = 3$

Which of the following concepts should Ms. Chavez review with this student?

A. order of operations

B. using inverse operations to solve an equation

C. combining like terms

D. subtraction

6

Which of the following is closest to 15,886 × 210?

A. 33,000

B. 330,000

C. 3,300,000

D. 33,000,000

7

A landscaping company charges 5 cents per square foot for fertilizer. How much would they charge to fertilize a 30-foot-by-50-foot lawn?

A. $7.50

B. $15.00

C. $75.00

D. $150.00

Use the following graph to answer questions 8 and 9.

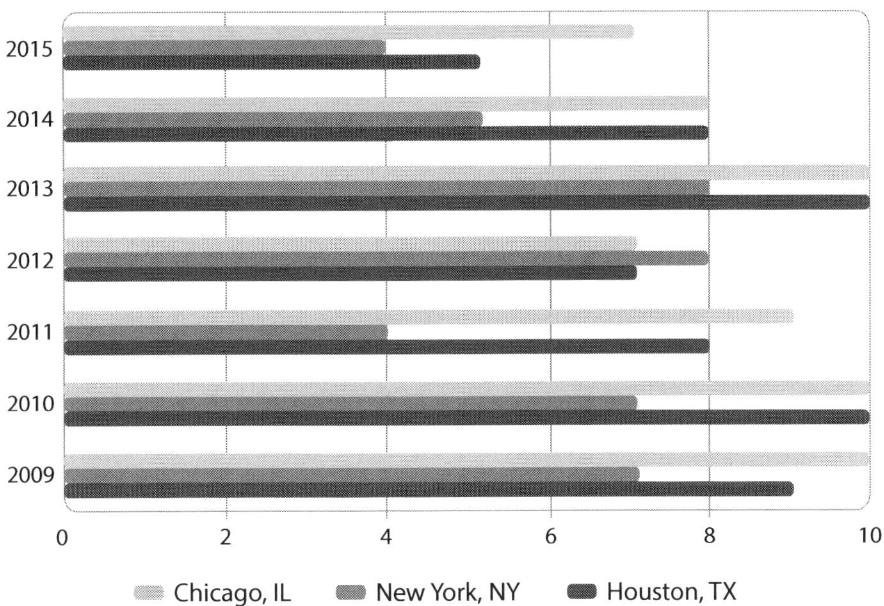

8

From 2009 to 2015, what is the average number of months that Chicago had 3 or less inches of rain?

A. 6

B. 7

C. 8

D. 9

9

New York had the fewest months with less than 3 inches of rain in every year EXCEPT:

A. 2012

B. 2013

C. 2014

D. 2015

10

Mr. Kahn gives the following problem to his students.

457 + 23 + 1092 =

Which of the following student answers is the result of aligning the addends at the left instead of aligning them at the right?

A. 1172

B. 1572

C. 7962

D. 141,612

11

Out of 1560 students at Ward Middle School, 15% want to take French. Which expression represents how many students want to take French?

A. $1560 \div 15$

B. 1560×15

C. 1560×0.15

D. $1560 \div 0.15$

12

A fourth-grade class is practicing rounding. Kevin's work is shown below.

> Round 4127.39 to the nearest tenth.
>
> <u>4130.00</u>

Which of the following most likely explains Kevin's error?

A. Kevin does not know which place value is referenced when rounding.

B. Kevin does not know the place value names.

C. Kevin does not understand when to round up versus when to round down.

D. Kevin does not understand how to decompose numbers.

13

Which digit is in the hundredths place when 1.3208 is divided by 5.2?

A. 0

B. 4

C. 5

D. 8

14

Which of the following is equivalent to (52 – 2)2 + 33 ?

A. 25

B. 30

C. 556

D. 538

15

Students board a bus at 7:45 a.m. and arrive at school at 8:20 a.m. How long are the students on the bus?

A. 30 minutes

B. 35 minutes

C. 45 minutes

D. 60 minutes

16

Which of the following operations could be used to introduce students to the concept of regrouping? Select all that apply.

A. 75 – 22

B. 219 – 108

C. 509 – 367

D. 694 – 292

17

A teacher has 50 notebooks to hand out to students. If she has 16 students in her class, and each student receives 2 notebooks, how many notebooks will she have left over?

A. 2

B. 16

C. 18

D. 32

18

What is the remainder when 397 is divided by 4?

A. 0

B. 1

C. 2

D. 4

19

A mode is the most frequently occurring value or values in a data set. Which of the following is an important characteristic of the mode that should be presented to students learning the concept?

A. A number not included in the data set can be the mode.

B. There can be more than one mode.

C. The mode is always the largest value in a data set.

D. The mode is always the middle value in a data set.

20

Solve for x: $5x - 4 = 3(8 + 3x)$

A. -7

B. $-\frac{3}{4}$

C. $\frac{3}{4}$

D. 7

21

If the value of y is between 0.0047 and 0.0162, which of the following could be the value of y?

A. 0.0035

B. 0.0055

C. 0.0185

D. 0.0238

22

Which three-dimensional solid has 2 triangular faces and 3 rectangular faces?

A. pyramid

B. cube

C. rectangular prism

D. triangular prism

23

A sixth-grade class is divided into groups and asked to collect quantitative data for a class project. Each group submits its plan to the teacher. Which group will need to be redirected?

A. group A: test scores of students in a class

B. group B: costs of different airline fares

C. group C: income of people in a company

D. group D: the favorite color of members in a family

24

W, X, Y, and Z lie on a circle with center A. If the diameter of the circle is 75, what is the sum of $\overline{AW}$, $\overline{AX}$, $\overline{AY}$, and $\overline{AZ}$?

A. 75

B. 106.5

C. 150

D. 300

25

Mr. Costas asked his students to decompose the number 27,358. Which of the following students decomposed the number properly?

A. Carly: 20,000 + 73 + 58

B. Jamey: 2,000 + 700 + 30 + 58

C. Taylor: 2 + 7 + 3 + 5 + 8

D. Andre: 20,000 + 7,000 + 300 + 50 + 8

26

The measures of two angles of a triangle are 25° and 110°. What is the measure of the third angle?

A. 40°

B. 45°

C. 50°

D. 55°

27

What is the perimeter of the shape below if each side is the same length?

A. 2 mm

B. 4 mm

C. 10 mm

D. 20 mm

28

Miguel usually receives a $5 allowance each week and currently has $10 saved. If he does not receive his allowance the next week, he will have $10 when that week is over.

Which of the following properties is demonstrated by this scenario?

A. identity property

B. commutative property

C. distributive property

D. associative property

30

Mrs. Lopez's class is learning to compare fractions. A student writes the following:

$\frac{5}{12}$ is greater than $\frac{5}{7}$ because 12 is greater than 7.

Which of the following is a correct assessment of the student's work?

A. The student is correct because 12 is greater than 7.

B. The student is correct because five parts out of twelve (5/12) is greater than five parts out of seven (5/7).

C. The student is incorrect because the numerators are the same, meaning the fractions are equal.

D. The student is incorrect because five parts out of twelve (5/12) is less than five parts out of seven (5/7).

29

Students are asked if they prefer vanilla, chocolate, or strawberry ice cream. The results are tallied on the table below.

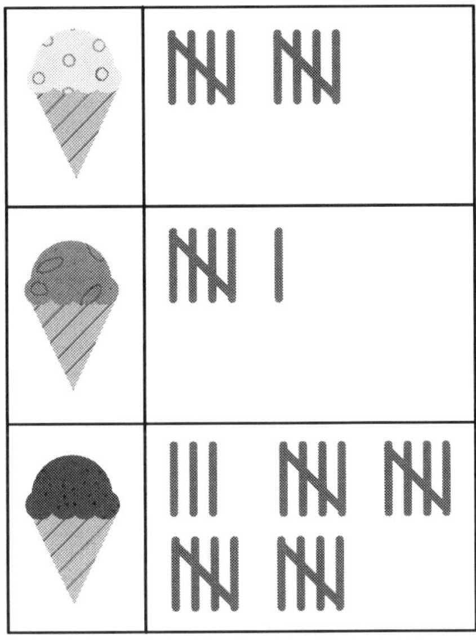

The students display the information from the table in a bar graph. Which student completes the bar graph correctly?

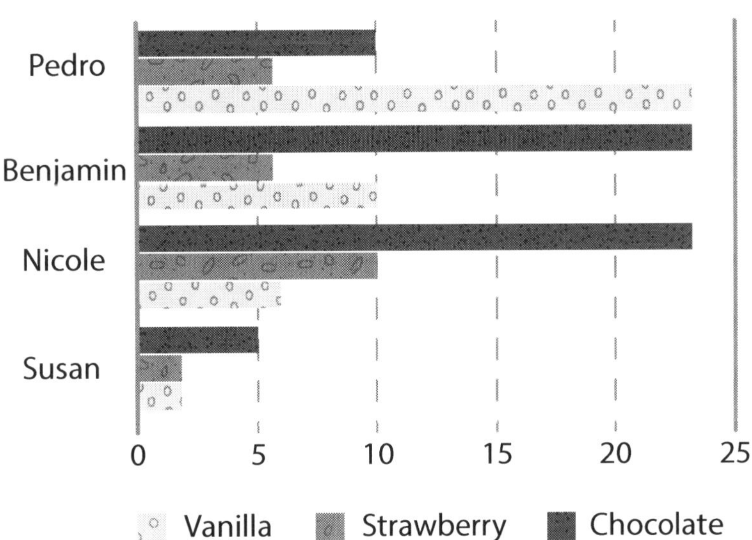

A. Pedro
B. Benjamin
C. Nicole
D. Susan

Writing

Read the question, and then choose the most correct answer.

1

Which of the following sentence errors is labeled CORRECTLY?

A. Since she went to the store. (fused)

B. The football game ended in a tie, the underdog caught up in the fourth quarter. (fragment)

C. The football game ended in a tie the underdog caught up in the fourth quarter. (fused)

D. When the players dropped their gloves, a fight broke out on the ice hockey rink floor. (comma splice)

2

Identify the error in the sentence.

Edward Jenner, (A)<u>considered</u> the father of immunology, invented the (B)<u>world's</u> first vaccine (C) <u>over infecting</u> a young boy with cowpox, successfully protecting him from the widespread (D), and far more dangerous, smallpox virus.

3

Which of the following situations requires passive listening?

A. sitting in the audience at an assembly

B. having a conversation with a friend

C. a waiter or waitress taking an order at a restaurant

D. having a conversation with a boss on how to improve job performance

4

A complex sentence must contain which of the following?

A. comma

B. coordinating conjunction

C. determiner

D. subordinate conjunction

5

A paraprofessional is asked to help choose texts for appropriateness for a first-grader who needs extra help with reading. Which of the following types of sentences should make up the majority of the text she chooses?

A. complex

B. compound

C. simple

D. compound-complex

6

Which of the following punctuation marks is used INCORRECTLY?

Our professor says that, though the term *nomad* is often associated with early populations, nomadic cultures exist today, especially in the mountain's of Europe and Asia.

A. the comma after *that*

B. the comma after *populations*

C. the comma after *today*

D. the apostrophe in *mountain's*

7

Identify the error in the sentence.

Ukrainians (A)<u>celebrate</u> a holiday called Malanka during which men (B)<u>dress in</u> costumes and masks and (C)<u>plays</u> tricks on (D)<u>their</u> neighbors.

8

Which of the following is the goal of active listening?

A. to give the appearance of disinterest in the speaker

B. to ensure that the listener has understood the speaker

C. to ask frequent and probing questions of the speaker

D. to be a good audience member during an oral presentation

9

Which of the following is NOT a way to correctly punctuate a compound sentence?

A. comma and subordinate conjunction

B. comma and coordinating conjunction

C. semicolon

D. colon

10

In the sentence, what word is an interjection?

Oh, I didn't hear you come in!

A. in

B. oh

C. hear

D. you

11

The <u>wood</u> stove overheated in the little cabin, so the smoke filled the main room.

In the sentence, the underlined word is being used as

A. a noun

B. a pronoun

C. an adjective

D. an adverb

12

Identify the error in the sentence.

(A)<u>Because of</u> (B)<u>it's</u> distance from the sun, the planet Neptune (C)<u>has seasons</u> that last the (D) <u>equivalent of</u> forty-one Earth years.

13

Which of the following is the first oral presentation many students give during their school career?

A. the first oral report a teacher assigns

B. the first time a teacher asks a new student to get up and introduce herself

C. their first experience with show and tell

D. a monologue they read

14

Identify the error in the sentence.

Everyday items like potatoes, (A) <u>bread,</u> onions, and even saliva (B) <u>is</u> the tools of art conservators, (C) <u>who</u> work to (D)<u>clean and restore</u> works of art.

15

A paraprofessional is assisting a teacher lead a third-grade class in a letter writing campaign to the city council in an effort to convince them not to tear down the Eleventh Street Park. Which of the following types of writing are the students participating in?

A. descriptive

B. cause and effect

C. compare and contrast

D. persuasive

16

We will move to Arizona <u>if</u> Dave continues to struggle with asthma.

In the sentence, the underlined word is being used as

A. a preposition

B. an adverb

C. a conjunction

D. an interjection

17

An elementary student writes the following sentences:

I gave my sister a gift. My sister asks if you know what it is.

Which of the following concepts should the paraprofessional review with the student?

A. sentence fragments

B. shifts in pronoun person

C. lack of pronoun agreement

D. use of a pronoun without an antecedent

18

Identify the error in the sentence.

As juveniles (A)<u>,</u> (B)<u>african</u> white-backed vultures are (C)<u>darkly</u> colored, developing their white feathers only as they (D)<u>grow into</u> adulthood.

19

Several administrators <u>did</u> understand the proposal, but most of them voted against the proposal.

In the sentence, the underlined word is being used as

A. a conjunction

B. a pronoun

C. a verb

D. an adverb

20

A paraprofessional is asked to help a second-grade student work on forming the past tense of verbs. Which of the following would be the most appropriate writing assignment to ensure sufficient practice with this skill?

A. writing a compare/contrast paragraph about cars and trucks

B. writing a paragraph about what they did over the winter break

C. writing a description of their living room

D. writing a persuasive paragraph about their favorite color

21

Identify the error in the sentence.

The Akhal-Teke horse breed, originally (A)from Turkmenistan, (B)have long enjoyed (C)a reputation for (D)bravery and fortitude.

22

In the sentence, the prefix *pre–* indicates that the evaluation will take place at which of the following times?

The patient's preoperative evaluation is scheduled for next Wednesday.

A. before the operation

B. after the operation

C. during the operation

D. at the end of the operation

23

A paraprofessional is reading a story with a small group of students in a second-grade class. He wants to emphasize that the narrator has a different point of view from the other characters. Which of the following should he do to emphasize this point?

A. read the entire story himself and point out when the narrator is speaking

B. have the students read in a different voice when reading/speaking as the narrator versus when reading/speaking as the characters

C. have students label the text for each line that is spoken by the narrator

D. have students read very slowly when reading the narrator's lines so that they can really appreciate his points

24

Identify the error in the sentence.

The employer (A)decided that he could not, (B)due to the high cost of health care, afford (C)to offer (D)no other benefits to his employees.

25

Which of the following is a complex sentence?

A. Engineers designed seat belts to stop the inertia of traveling bodies by applying an opposing force to the driver and passengers during a collision.

B. Hurricanes cost the United States roughly $5 billion per year in damages and have been the cause of almost two million deaths in the last two hundred years.

C. Woodstock appeared in the *Peanuts* comic strips as early as April 1967, but he was not named until June 1970, ten months after the famous music festival of the same name, Woodstock.

D. Although organized firefighting groups existed as early as ancient Egyptian times, the first fully state-run brigade was created by Emperor Augustus of Rome.

26

Identify the error in the sentence.

Though Puerto Rico is known popularly for (A)its beaches, its landscape also (B)include mountains, which (C)are home to many of the (D)island's rural villages.

27

In a third-grade class, the students are working on research projects and have been asked to focus on three sub-topics that they will investigate. Marissa, who has selected *dance* as her research topic, is having a hard time coming up with three sub-topics.

Which of the following is the best way for the paraprofessional to help Marissa come up with three sub-topics?

A. ask Marissa when she started dancing and why she likes it so much

B. suggest Marissa change her topic if she can't find three sub-topics

C. ask Marissa what types of dance she likes and have her conduct an online encyclopedic search (from trusted sites) for types of dance

D. have Marissa do a freewriting exercise in which she writes down a word web of all of the terms she associates with dance

28

Which of the following nouns is written in the CORRECT plural form?

A. shelves

B. phenomenons

C. mans

D. deers

29

Which of the following parts of speech is *travels* as used in the sentence?

Abby's travels in Asia provided her the opportunity to try many foods that she would not have been able to try at home in the United States.

A. verb

B. noun

C. adjective

D. adverb

30

Which of the following types of text would most likely contain a moral?

A. a descriptive essay

B. a compare/contrast essay

C. a fairy tale

D. a newspaper article

Answer Key

Reading

1)

A. **Correct.** Understanding that words are what is read on a page is an important part of print awareness.

B. Incorrect. This would help the paraprofessional, not necessarily Henry; furthermore, the paraprofessional likely has another reason for her actions.

C. Incorrect. This would not necessarily help lull him to sleep.

D. Incorrect. It is unlikely that Henry is able to read the words.

2)

A. Incorrect. The passage does not describe the actual artwork at all.

B. Incorrect. The author names the artist who made the painting, but states nothing else about its origin.

C. Incorrect. While the author does state that there are four versions of the artwork, this is not the primary purpose of the passage.

D. **Correct.** The author writes, "*The Scream of Nature* by Edvard Munch is one of the world's best known and most desirable artworks."

3)

A. Incorrect. A poetry anthology is a collection of poems.

B. Incorrect. A short story is a short work of fiction.

C. Incorrect. A novel is a long work of fiction.

D. **Correct.** A brochure is a non-fiction text without characters that provides the reader with information about a given topic.

4)

A. **Correct.** The author goes on to describe the shared perspectives of these writers.

B. Incorrect. The author does not indicate the number of writers.

C. Incorrect. The author provides no context that implies they were an organized group, simply that they shared certain traits.

D. Incorrect. The author states that they gathered in one place—Paris.

5)

A. Incorrect. Phonemic awareness is understanding how phonemes create differences in word meaning. Rene's actions show she needs a better understanding of concepts of print rather than phonemic awareness.

B. Incorrect. Phonological awareness is the understanding of how sounds, sounds, syllables, words, and word parts can be orally manipulated to break apart words, make new words, and create rhymes. Rene needs more practice with concepts of print, not understanding how sounds can become words.

C. Incorrect. Letter-sound correspondence describes how letters relate to the spoken sounds in words. Rene is confused about concepts of print.

D. **Correct.** Rene understands that books are to be read, but she may not yet understand that they have a clear order of beginning, middle, and end.

6)

A. Incorrect. The author writes that the officers, not the volunteers, were veterans.

B. Incorrect. The passage does not mention a citizenship requirement.

C. Incorrect. While most of the volunteers were indeed from the Southwest, the passage does not say this was a requirement.

D. **Correct.** The author writes, "the army set high standards: all of the recruits had to be skilled on horseback…"

7)

A. Incorrect. Mark knows the individual sound of each letters, so he understands the alphabetic principle.

B. Incorrect. This word does not have a prefix or suffix.

C. **Correct.** Mark did not sound out the word into onset *fl* and rime *at*.

D. Incorrect. Mark sounded the blend *fl* as two individual sounds *f-l*, so he does not seem to have a strong familiarity with it.

8)

A. Incorrect. While the author does describe his memory loss, this is not the main idea of the passage.

B. **Correct.** The author writes, "From this, scientists learned that different types of memory are handled by different parts of the brain."

C. Incorrect. The author does explain the differences in long-term and short-term memory formation, but not until the end of the passage.

D. Incorrect. While it is implied that memories of physical skills are processed differently than memories of events, this is not the main idea of the passage.

9)

A. Incorrect. Beech trees are not included in the list of species found in tropical rain forests.

B. Incorrect. Beech trees are not included in the list of species found in temperate deciduous forests.

C. **Correct.** Beech trees are included in the list of species found in temperate deciduous forests.

D. Incorrect. Beech trees are not included in the list of species found in temperate coniferous forests.

10)

A. Incorrect. This is a question about character motivation, not point of view.

B. **Correct.** If the student answers correctly, he will have identified the dinosaur as the first-person narrator protagonist

C. Incorrect. This is a question about setting.

D. Incorrect. This might help establish the student's point of view toward the story, but it does not address the first-person point of view within the story.

11)

A. Incorrect. The author does not provide enough detailed evidence to reasonably infer the Confederate reaction to the march.

B. Correct. The author describes the level of destruction in detail, suggesting it had a significant negative impact on the Confederacy.

C. Incorrect. Again, as in option *A*, the author does not describe any response to the march.

D. Incorrect. The author writes, "Sherman estimated his troops inflicted $100 million in damages."

12)

A. Correct. This defines the plot of a fiction work.

B. Incorrect. This defines the climax.

C. Incorrect. This defines the conflict.

D. Incorrect. This defines the setting.

13)

A. Incorrect. The author discusses plans to study magnetic and gravitational fields on Saturn, not Titan.

B. Incorrect. The author writes, "Then it will pass through the unexplored region between Saturn itself and its famous rings." The passage does not mention any rings on Titan.

C. Correct. The author writes, "…it will record any changes in Titan's curious methane lakes, providing information about potential seasons on the planet-sized moon."

D. Incorrect. The author refers to the rings of Saturn, not to Titan, when stating, "Scientists hope to learn how old the rings are."

14)

A. Incorrect. Phonological awareness should be mastered before phonics instruction.

B. Correct. Memorizing sight words through multiple exposures will help students read more quickly and fluently.

C. Incorrect. Concepts of print teach students about the structures of reading materials; they do not improve reading fate and fluency.

D. Incorrect. Spelling will not help with reading rate and fluency.

15)

A. Correct. The author writes, "a shoelace knot experiences greater g-force than any rollercoaster can generate," helping the reader understand the strength of the g-force experienced by the knots.

B. Incorrect. The author does not describe any actual experiments involving rollercoasters.

C. Incorrect. The author does not assess the findings of the experiment.

D. Incorrect. The rollercoaster reference is a comparison, not specific evidence.

16)

A. Correct. Phonemic awareness does not come naturally. This is why people who cannot read can still use oral language.

B. Incorrect. Phonemic awareness must be taught.

C. Incorrect. Students will develop phonemic awareness at a different speed based on many factors.

D. Incorrect. Students need to be able to understand and use sounds to sound out words and read.

17)

A. Incorrect. The author implies that bedbugs transitioned to humans relatively easily.

B. Incorrect. The author does not address the impact of light on bedbugs.

C. Correct. The author writes, "Humans only lived seasonally in the Oregon cave system, however, which might explain why these insects did not fully transfer to human hosts like bedbugs elsewhere did."

D. Incorrect. The author does not address the growth rate of bedbug populations.

18)

A. Correct. The diner has the fewest number of bacon slices (nineteen), and bacon slices occupy the smallest slice of the pie chart.

B. Incorrect. According to the pie chart, Gigi's diner has thirty-seven cheese slices, whereas it only has nineteen bacon slices.

C. Incorrect. The pie chart shows that the diner has eighty hamburger buns, which is far more than the nineteen bacon slices it has.

D. Incorrect. Gigi's has 200 hamburger patties, its largest stock of food.

19)

A. Correct. Adding 120 buns to the existing eighty buns would provide enough buns for 200 hamburgers.

B. Incorrect. Adding 161 buns to the stock of eighty buns would result in 241 buns, leaving a surplus of forty-one buns.

C. Incorrect. Adding 181 buns to the stock of eighty buns would result in 261 buns, leaving a surplus of sixty-one buns.

D. Incorrect. Adding 200 buns to the stock of eighty buns would result in 280 buns, leaving a surplus of eighty buns.

20)

A. Correct. There are enough bacon slices to make nineteen burgers, and enough cheese slices to make eighteen burgers ($37 \div 2 = 18.5$). The most hamburgers that Gigi's could make would be eighteen.

B. Incorrect. There is not enough cheese to make nineteen burgers with two cheese slices each.

C. Incorrect. There is not enough cheese or bacon to make thirty-nine burgers.

D. Incorrect. While there are exactly eighty buns, there is not enough cheese or bacon to make eighty burgers with cheese and bacon.

21)

A. Incorrect. While this is stated in the first sentence, it is not the main idea.

B. Correct. The passage describes the origin of Yellowstone's geysers.

C. Incorrect. While the author states this in the passage, it is not the main idea.

D. Incorrect. This is not stated in the passage.

22)

A. Incorrect. This question would guide the student towards an understanding of characters.

B. Incorrect. Pre-kindergarten students likely would not understand the word *resolved*, and this question helps guide towards an understanding of resolution, not conflict.

C. Correct. This question is age-appropriate, and would help the student identify the conflict.

D. Incorrect. This question would help the student identify the setting.

23)

A. Incorrect. The pronoun *he* is associated with the third-person point of view.

B. Incorrect. The pronoun *I* is associated with the first-person point of view.

C. Incorrect. The pronoun *us* is associated with the first-person point of view.

D. Correct. The pronoun *you* is associated with the second-person point of view.

24)

A. Incorrect. This activity will not help Anna catch up with the class at all.

B. Incorrect. Anna is likely not ready for this exercise if she is not yet familiar with basic phonemes.

C. Incorrect. While the paraprofessional can assist Anna in building her English vocabulary, Anna can participate in phonics activities if they are modified appropriately.

D. Correct. Anna is likely not familiar with many of the forty-four phonemes of English, and she will need practice with these before tackling more advanced activities such as the consonant digraphs the rest of the class is working on. The paraprofessional can assist Anna in learning basic English phonemes.

25)

A. Incorrect. While the text does list several family members of Custer who died in the battle, this is not the main idea.

B. Correct. The author writes, "the allied tribes decisively defeated their US foes."

C. Incorrect. The author does not explain why the cavalry was formed.

D. Incorrect. The author does not describe the personal relationship between Sitting Bull and Custer.

26)

A. Incorrect. Generally a narrative in the first-person point of view features the author as the main character or protagonist.

B. Incorrect. In first person point of view, the author is generally the narrator/protagonist, and the reader knows what he or she is thinking.

C. Correct. This is the characteristic of many narratives written in first person point of view.

D. Incorrect. This is third person omniscient point of view.

27)

A. Incorrect. Lexile charts deal with the readability of texts.

B. Incorrect. Flesch-Kincaid also deals with readability of texts and is not a list.

C. Correct. This list of 315 words contains the most frequently used words in English.

D. Incorrect. This is not a sight word list.

28)

A. Incorrect. According to the index, the entry for explicit memory begins on page 316.

B. Incorrect. The index states that the entry for implicit memory begins on page 319.

C. Incorrect. Page 333 is where the entry for long-term memory can be found.

D. Correct. The index indicates that the entry for short-term memory begins on page 340.

29)

A. Incorrect. The story has already built the anticipation.

B. Correct. The paraprofessional is helping the student guess what might happen in the story.

C. Incorrect. The paraprofessional is assisting the teacher in integrating the curriculum by reading the book; the student is not integrating the curriculum.

D. Incorrect. This question does not ask about character motivation.

30)

A. Incorrect. The author provides no evidence that invasive species typically help native species.

B. Incorrect. The author writes that the quagga mussels, an invasive species, harmed native species.

C. Incorrect. The author implies that quagga mussels are thriving.

D. Correct. The author writes that "the reason for the cisco's reemergence is even more unlikely. The cisco have an invasive species, quagga mussels, to thank for their return."

MATHEMATICS

1)

D. **Correct.** Add zeros as needed so that each number is expressed in thousandths; then add the numbers.

$951.400 + 98.908 + 1.053 =$

$1{,}051.361 \rightarrow$ **7 digits**

2)

B. **Correct.** Rather than getting a common denominator and adding numerators, the student merely added both numerators and denominators. Based on that reasoning, the student would write that $\frac{1}{3} + \frac{1}{2} = \mathbf{\frac{2}{5}}$

3)

B. **Correct.** Because the answer choices all use the same digits, the problem can be solved using estimation.

$100 \div 30 \approx 3$, so **3.41** is the best answer.

4)

D. **Correct.** Find the least common denominator, and then add the whole numbers and fractions separately.

LCD = 8

that $1\frac{3}{4} + 2\frac{3}{8} =$

$1\frac{6}{8} + 2\frac{3}{8} = 3\frac{9}{8} = \mathbf{4\frac{1}{8}}$

5)

C. **Correct.** Leslie is attempting to combine terms that are not like terms.

6)

C. **Correct.** Round each number and multiply.

$16{,}000 \times 200 = 3{,}200{,}000 \rightarrow$ close to **3,300,000**

7)

C. **Correct.** Multiply the area by the charge per square foot.

Area = $50 \times 30 = 1{,}500$ square feet

$1{,}500 \times 0.05 =$ **\$75.00**

8)

D. **Correct.** Use the graph to find the number of months Chicago had less than 3 inches of rain year, and then find the average.

months with < 3 inches rain in Chicago: {7, 8, 10, 7, 9, 10, 10}

$\frac{7 + 8 + 10 + 7 + 9 + 10 + 10}{7} = 8.7 \approx \mathbf{9}$

9)

A. **Correct.** In 2012, New York had more months with less than 3 inches of rain than either Chicago or Houston.

10)

C. **Correct.** The work below shows the incorrect answer resulting from aligning the numbers on the left.

$$\begin{array}{l} 457 \\ 23 \\ \underline{+\,1092} \\ \mathbf{7962} \end{array}$$

11)

C. **Correct.** Use the formula for finding percentages. Express the percentage as a decimal.

part = *whole* × *percentage* =

$\mathbf{1560 \times 0.15}$

12)

B. **Correct.** Kevin rounded to the tens place instead of the tenths place.

13)

C. **Correct.** Divide 1.3208 by 5.2.

There is a **5** in the hundredths place.

14)

C. **Correct.** Simplify using PEMDAS.

(52 – 2)2 + 33

= (25 – 2)2 + 33

= (23)2 + 33

= 529 + 27 = **556**

15)

B. **Correct.** There are 15 minutes between 7:45 a.m. and 8:00 a.m. and 20 minutes between 8:00 a.m. and 8:20 a.m.

15 minutes + 20 minutes =

35 minutes

16)

C. **Correct.** 509 – 367 requires regrouping in the tens place because 6 is greater than 0. The other choices do not require regrouping.

17)

C. **Correct.** If each student receives 2 notebooks, the teacher will need 16 × 2 = 32 notebooks. After handing out the notebooks, she will have 50 – 32 = **18 notebooks left**.

18)

B. **Correct.** Find the highest possible multiple of 4 that is less than or equal to 397, and then subtract to find the remainder.

$99 \times 4 = 396$

$397 - 396 = \mathbf{1}$

19)

B. **Correct.** Since there can be several data values that occur at the same frequency, there can be more than one mode. The other statements are false.

20)

A. **Correct.** Isolate the variable x on one side of the equation.

$5x - 4 = 3(8 + 3x)$

$5x - 4 = 24 + 9x$

$-4 - 24 = 9x - 5x$

$-28 = 4x$

$\frac{-28}{4} = \frac{4x}{4}$

$\mathbf{x = -7}$

21)

B. **Correct.** All of the decimal numbers are expressed in ten-thousandths. 55 is between 47 and 162, so **0.0055** is between 0.0047 and 0.0162.

22)

D. **Correct.** Only a triangular prism has 2 triangular faces and 3 rectangular faces. There are no rectangular faces on a pyramid. There are no triangular faces on a cube or on a rectangular prism.

23)

D. **Correct.** Since color is a physical characteristic, it is a qualitative observation. The other choices are all numeric, or quantitative, qualities.

24)

C. **Correct.** All the points lie on the circle, so each line segment is a radius. The sum of the 4 lines will be 4 times the radius.

$r = \frac{75}{2} = 37.5$

$4r = \mathbf{150}$

25)

A. Incorrect. Carly did not completely decompose the number.

B. Incorrect. Jamey incorrectly identified the place value of the digits.

C. Incorrect. Taylor added the digits.

D. **Correct.** Andre broke down the number into its individual place values.

26)

B. **Correct.** The sum of the measures of the three angles in a triangle is 180°. Subtract the two given angle measures from 180 to find the measure of the third angle.

$180° - 25° - 110° = \mathbf{45°}$

27)

D. **Correct.** To find the perimeter, add the length of each side to find the total.

$P = 2(10) = \mathbf{20\ mm}$

28)

A. **Correct.** Miguel started with $10 and did not receive his allowance: 10 + 0 = 10. This scenario describes the additive property of identity.

29)

A. Incorrect. Pedro's graph is incorrect. He confuses the number of students who prefer vanilla with the number of students who prefer chocolate.

B. **Correct.** Benjamin completed the graph correctly. His bar graph indicates that 10 students prefer vanilla, 6 students prefer strawberry, and 23 students prefer chocolate ice cream.

C. Incorrect. Nicole did not complete the graph correctly. She confuses the number of students who like vanilla with the number of students who like strawberry.

D. Incorrect. Susan's graph is not correct. She did not accurately count the tallies before making her bar graph.

30)

A. Incorrect. Fractions are not compared by comparing just the denominators.

B. Incorrect. Five parts out of twelve (5/12) is not greater than five parts out of seven (5/7).

C. Incorrect. The numerators are the same, but the denominators are not, so the fractions are not equal.

D. **Correct.** Five parts out of twelve (5/12) is less than five parts out of seven (5/7).

Writing

1)

A. Incorrect. This is a fragment: it is a dependent clause with no independent clause accompanying it.

B. Incorrect. This is a comma splice. To connect the two independent clauses, it needs a preposition such as *with* following the comma.

C. **Correct.** In this sentence, two independent clauses are fused: there is no punctuation where the two clauses meet.

D. Incorrect. This is not a comma splice, but the sentence does not make good sense. *When* should be deleted, *the* should be capitalized, and a conjunction such as *and* should be inserted following the comma.

2)

A. Incorrect. *Considered* begins an adjectival phrase that describes the subject of the sentence (Jenner).

B. Incorrect. *World's* must be possessive, as it refers to the first vaccine *of* the world.

C. **Correct.** The preposition *over* does not accurately illustrate the relationship between the vaccine and the young boy's infection; more appropriate would be the preposition *by*.

D. Incorrect. The comma after *widespread* is needed to set off the appositive phrase *and far more dangerous*.

3)

A. **Correct.** Passive listening calls for the listener to listen without conversing.

B. Incorrect. This situation calls for active listening; to hold a conversation, one must speak back.

C. Incorrect. This calls for active listening as the waiter or waitress will need to confirm understanding with the customer.

D. Incorrect. This calls for active listening in order to have a productive conversation.

4)

A. Incorrect. A dependent clause does not always need a comma when joined to an independent clause to form a complex sentence.

B. Incorrect. A coordinating conjunction would be most likely to be found in a compound sentence.

C. Incorrect. A complex sentence does not necessarily need a determiner which tells what a noun refers to.

D. **Correct.** A complex sentence contains a dependent clause which is introduced by a subordinate conjunction.

5)

A. Incorrect. A text composed mostly of complex sentences would be quite difficult for first-graders.

B. Incorrect. Reading selections made up mainly of compound sentences would be too advanced for first-graders.

C. **Correct.** To be appropriate for a first-grade class, most of the sentences should be simple sentences consisting of a single independent clause.

D. Incorrect. Passages composed mainly of compound-complex sentences would be too complicated for most first-graders, and thus are not developmentally appropriate.

6)

A. Incorrect. This comma and the one following populations are correctly used to set off the phrase *though the term...populations*.

B. Incorrect. This comma is used correctly to connect a dependent clause to an independent one.

C. Incorrect. This comma is used correctly to indicate a pause.

D. **Correct.** *Mountain's* is not possessive in this sentence. It functions as a plural noun (*mountains*) so it does not require an apostrophe.

7)

A. Incorrect. *Celebrate* provides a plural verb for the plural subject *Ukrainians*.

B. Incorrect. *Dress* is a singular, present-tense verb that agrees with its subject (*men*) and the rest of the sentence (*celebrate*); *in* is the appropriate preposition to complete the idiom *dress in*, meaning "wear."

C. **Correct.** *Plays* is a singular verb and does not correctly pair with the plural subject *men*; *men dress* and *play*.

D. Incorrect. *Their* is a possessive pronoun describing whose neighbors are being referred to in the sentence (*the men's*).

8)

A. Incorrect. In active listening, one listens intently and with interest.

B. **Correct.** This is the ultimate goal of active listening to promote better oral communication.

C. Incorrect. This does not promote understanding necessarily and may disrupt the speaker.

D. Incorrect. Generally, being an audience member calls for passive listening.

9)

A. **Correct.** A subordinate conjunction, either with or without a comma dependent upon the purpose and placement of the clause, is used with a complex sentence, not a compound sentence.

B. Incorrect. A comma and a coordinating conjunction (and, but, or, nor, for, yet) is one correct way to punctuate a compound sentence.

C. Incorrect. A semicolon can be used to correctly join two closely related independent clauses into a compound sentence

D. Incorrect. A colon can also be used to correctly join two independent clauses when the second clause is an elaboration or example of the first clause.

10)

A. Incorrect. *In* is a preposition.

B. **Correct.** *Oh* is an interjection.

C. Incorrect. *Hear* is a verb.

D. Incorrect. *You* is a pronoun.

11)

A. Incorrect. In this sentence, *wood* is a modifying noun, which becomes an adjective in usage.

B. Incorrect. Here, *wood* does not take the place of a noun.

C. **Correct.** In this sentence, *wood* describes the type of stove (wood stove, electric stove, gas stove).

D. Incorrect. The word *wood* is modifying a noun, not a verb, adjective, adverb, or entire sentence.

12)

A. Incorrect. *Because of* is an introductory phrase that accurately describes the relationship between a cause (Neptune's distance from the sun) and its effect (length of seasons).

B. **Correct.** *It's* is a contraction of *it is*. The possessive pronoun *its* is required here to describe Neptune's distance from the sun.

C. Incorrect. *Has* is a singular verb, referring to a singular noun (Neptune); *seasons* is the direct object of the verb *has*.

D. Incorrect. As a noun, *equivalent* is typically followed by *of* (the equivalent of something); as a verb, *equivalent* is usually followed by *to* (something is equivalent to something else).

13)

A. Incorrect. Students usually complete a formal oral report long after their first experiences with show and tell.

B. Incorrect. Show and tell typically predates this.

C. **Correct.** Show and tell is a great early introduction to giving and listening to an oral presentation.

D. Incorrect. Show and tell usually comes first.

14)

A. Incorrect. *Bread* is correctly punctuated in this sentence; it is followed by a comma to offset it from the next item in the list, *onions*.

B. **Correct.** The verb in this sentence (*is*) must be edited in order to create agreement between the subject (*items like potatoes, bread, onions, and even saliva*) and the verb (which should be *are*).

C. Incorrect. *Who* is the subjective form of the pronoun, used here to describe the noun *art conservators*.

D. Incorrect. *Clean and restore* is a compound verb phrase; both verbs are correctly formatted as plural.

15)

A. Incorrect. Descriptive writing describes something.

B. Incorrect. She is not necessarily asking her students to write about a cause and effect.

C. Incorrect. Her class is not telling how anything is both alike and different.

D. **Correct.** She is asking the class to write to persuade the city council to keep the park open.

16)

A. Incorrect. Here, *if* does not come before an object and is not used as a preposition.

B. Incorrect. The word *if* does not modify a verb, adjective, adverb, or entire sentence.

C. **Correct.** The word *if* introduces an adverb clause, a dependent clause. Subordinating conjunctions introduce adverb clauses.

D. Incorrect. The word *if* does not express strong emotion and does have a grammatical role.

17)

A. Incorrect. Both of these are sentences.

B. **Correct.** The student has unnecessarily shifted to the second person "you" when there is no need for such a shift.

C. Incorrect. All of the pronouns agree with their antecedents.

D. Incorrect. It is clear that *it* refers back to *gift*.

18)

A. Incorrect. The comma is used correctly here to set off an introductory phrase (*as juveniles*).

B. **Correct.** *African* is derived from the name of a place (Africa) and is therefore a proper noun and needs to be capitalized.

C. Incorrect. *Darkly* is an adverb describing the adjective *colored*.

D. Incorrect. *Grow into* is an idiomatic phrase that describes a transition.

19)

A. Incorrect. The word *did* is not joining words within the sentence.

B. Incorrect. The word *did* is not taking the place of a noun.

C. Correct. The word *did* is helping the main verb *understand* and expresses emphatic tense.

D. Incorrect. The word *did* is not modifying the main verb *understand*; *did* is part of the verb phrase.

20)

A. Incorrect. This assignment would most logically be in the present tense.

B. Correct. This assignment would most logically be written in the past tense and would provide practice with forming the past tense.

C. Incorrect. This assignment would most logically be written in the present tense.

D. Incorrect. This assignment would most logically be written in the present tense.

21)

A. Incorrect. *From* is an appropriate preposition in this context, as it describes the origin (*originally from*) of the horse breed.

B. Correct. The subject of this sentence is the singular *breed*; though it is separated from the subject by an adjectival phrase, the verb must also be singular (*has*).

C. Incorrect. *A reputation* is a singular noun, acting as the direct object; it should remain singular to show that one reputation is held by the breed as a whole.

D. Incorrect. *Bravery* and *fortitude* are grammatically similar nouns, both being used to name the qualities for which the breed is known.

22)

A. Correct. The prefix *pre–* means "before."

B. Incorrect. The prefix *pre–* does not mean "after."

C. Incorrect. The prefix *pre–* does not mean "during."

D. Incorrect. The prefix *pre–* does not mean "at the end of."

23)

A. Incorrect. This is not the best strategy and might bore the students somewhat.

B. Correct. This will help students begin to understand that the narrator is telling the story from a different point of view.

C. Incorrect. This is not a read-aloud activity

D. Incorrect. Read-alouds should always be designed to help increase fluency through rate, accuracy, and prosody.

24)

A. Incorrect. *Decided* is a past-tense verb, which matches the tense of the phrase *could not*.

B. Incorrect. *Due to* accurately describes the relationship between cause (*high cost of health care*) and effect (*could not...afford*).

C. Incorrect. *To offer* is an infinitive phrase, acting as the direct object of the complete verb phrase *could not afford*.

D. Correct. Because it is a negative, *no other* inaccurately discounts the first negative (*not*) and creates a double negative (*could not afford no other*); it should be changed to *any other*.

25)

A. Incorrect. This sentence has one independent clause; it has no dependent clauses.

B. Incorrect. This sentence has one subject and two predicates; it has no dependent clauses.

C. Incorrect. This sentence has two independent clauses connected by a comma and a conjunction.

D. **Correct.** The sentence has an independent clause (*the fully... of Rome*) and a dependent clause (*Although organized...Egyptian times*). The two are connected with a comma following the word *times*.

26)

A. Incorrect. *Its* is a singular possessive pronoun, used here to refer to the *beaches* of the singular subject *Puerto Rico*.

B. **Correct.** The subject of the verb *include* is the singular *landscape*, so the verb should be conjugated in the singular (*includes*).

C. Incorrect. *Are* is a plural verb for the plural subject *mountains*.

D. Incorrect. *Island's* is the singular possessive form of *island*, used here to refer to the *rural villages* of the singular *island* of Puerto Rico.

27)

A. Incorrect. This might help her think more deeply about the topic, but it won't necessarily help her decide on three sub-topics.

B. Incorrect. Dance is a good topic because it seems Marissa is interested in it. She just needs further prompting from the paraprofessional.

C. **Correct.** This is the second phase of the research process in which students find background information and conduct a preliminary search on their topic.

D. Incorrect. This is not part of the research process and seems more of a word-association activity which might lead to a descriptive, but not research, piece on this topic.

28)

A. **Correct.** The correct plural form of *shelf* is *shelves*.

B. Incorrect. The correct plural form of *phenomenon* is *phenomena*.

C. Incorrect. The correct plural form of *man* is *men*.

D. Incorrect. The correct plural form of *deer* is *deer*.

29)

A. Incorrect. *Travels* functions as a noun, not as a verb like *provided*.

B. **Correct.** *Travels* functions as a noun; it is the subject of the sentence.

C. Incorrect. *Travels* functions as a noun, not as an adjective like *spicy*.

D. Incorrect. *Travels* functions as a noun, not as an adverb like *adventurously*.

30)

A. Incorrect. A moral is a lesson to be learned, and this would not necessarily be found in a descriptive essay.

B. Incorrect. A compare/contrast essay would likely not contain a moral.

C. **Correct.** Many fairy tales contain lessons that students might take away. For example, the moral of *Beauty and the Beast* is not to judge someone based on outward appearance.

D. Incorrect. An expository newspaper article usually will not contain a moral.

To access your second ParaPro practice test, follow the link below:
www.cirrustestprep.com/parapro-online-resources.

Made in the USA
San Bernardino, CA
10 March 2020

65508971R00095